COAL WAR

—— IN THE ——

Mahoning Valley

COAL WAR

—— IN THE ——

Mahoning Valley

THE ORIGIN OF GREATER YOUNGSTOWN'S ITALIANS

Joe Tucciarone & Ben Lariccia

History
PRESS

Published by The History Press
Charleston, SC
www.historypress.com

Copyright © 2019 by Joe Tucciarone and Ben Lariccia
All rights reserved

On the Front Cover: Ohio, the mining troubles in Hocking Valley, scene in the town of Buchtel. The striking miners' reception of "Blackleg" workmen when returning from their work escorted by a detachment of Pinkerton's detectives. From a sketch by Joseph Becker; Hyde.

First published 2019

Manufactured in the United States

ISBN 9781467142724

Library of Congress Control Number: 2019935362

Notice: The information in this book is true and complete to the best of our knowledge. It is offered without guarantee on the part of the authors or The History Press. The authors and The History Press disclaim all liability in connection with the use of this book.

To Adeline (Tucciarone) Ackerman and Anna Mae (Tucciarone) Tomillo, whose detective work uncovered coal dust in the family tree; to Giuseppe Lariccia, whose ordeals in 1901 Youngstown echo in this account.

CONTENTS

Contents

CONTENTS

RECONSTRUCTING THE PAST

I grew up in the 1960s, and I remember Coalburg as a patchwork of small farms, like the one owned by my grandparents William and Mary Tucciarone. We went there almost every weekend, and highlights of a visit might include a climb in the barn or a ride on Grandpa's tractor. It was a quiet place where often the only sound you could hear was the wind in the trees. I had no idea that, almost a century earlier, Coalburg had been a lively community dominated by railroad barons, coal kings and iron moguls. In those days, a continuous stream of coal trains rumbled from its depot and thundered across the tracks to Youngstown, Ashtabula and Cleveland, while hundreds of miners labored ceaselessly in the dark pits beneath its fields. All this activity was driven by the vast mineral wealth that underlay Coalburg—for, as its name suggests, coal was its raison d'être.

Coal War in the Mahoning Valley grew out of my research into a saloon. In 1882, my great-grandfather Joe Madeline emigrated from Italy to the United States. Twenty years later, he was running a hotel and saloon, the Clover Leaf House, in my hometown of Hubbard, Ohio. The building still stands, just south of the railroad tracks on the north end of town. However, nobody seemed to know when he opened the business. This led me to search through the Trumbull County archives to see if I could find a deed for the lot. After spending six months paging through thousands of documents, I finally located the 1903 title for Joe's saloon. But long before that, I had uncovered the deed for a home he purchased in 1888. It was his very first property, and it was located not in Hubbard but in nearby Coalburg. More research showed that his first three sons were born in Coalburg. There was even a family legend that Joe had owned a coal mine. All of this led me to conclude that Coalburg, not Hubbard, was the first landfall of the Madeline family in the United States. And what about the coal mine? I returned to my research to find out more.

Eventually, Ben Lariccia and I uncovered a long-lost chapter of Coalburg's history from the early 1870s. This led to the discovery of forgotten records from other coal camps in the Youngstown area, including those at Church Hill in Liberty Township and Lisbon in Columbiana County. These documents revealed that, in the closing months of 1872, a slowing market for iron and rising tensions among Mahoning Valley miners—fueled by coal operators' decision to revoke a recent pay increase—precipitated a strike on New Year's Day 1873. The walkout of the Coalburg miners forced the tiny community onto the national stage. The resolution of the conflict set a precedent for labor practices that would haunt immigrant and native-born workers for decades. On March 19, 1873, the mine owners fired an opening volley against the rebellion. They brought a hundred Italian immigrants to Coalburg as strikebreakers. This was the earliest group of Italians to settle in the Mahoning Valley and the first wave of what later grew to be our large Italian American community.

—Joe Tucciarone

PREFACE

This study aims to push back the veil that obscures the Italian American community's origin in the Greater Youngstown area. The authors' research reveals the coal miners' strike of 1873 as the pivotal event that opened the Mahoning Valley to Italian settlement. In the following pages, readers will find evidence to confirm this claim. But why add to the record? Marcus Tullius Cicero said it best two thousand years ago: "To be ignorant of what occurred before you were born is to remain always a child. For what is the worth of human life, unless it is woven into the life of our ancestors by the records of history?"[1]

By the time of the U.S. Civil War, European immigrants constituted a growing number of residents in Ohio. Among the six counties forming the northeastern corner of the state—Lake, Ashtabula, Geauga, Portage, Trumbull and Mahoning—newcomers could be found from England, France, Ireland, Austria-Hungary, Germany and even far-off Russia. The region encompasses an area of 4,300 square miles, and in 1860, it had a total population of more than 140,000 people. Yet there is no evidence that a single Italian immigrant lived in those parts during this period.

When the census was taken a decade later, it showed that just three Italians had made their homes in the six-county area. One of these was Pietro Anghi, a butcher in the village of Franklin in Portage County. He lived next door to a grocer who, presumably, sold his cuts of meat. Another Italian immigrant mentioned in the census was a stonecutter named Frank Hill, who lived on a farm in Thompson Township in Geauga County.

Meanwhile, in Trumbull County, a twenty-four-year-old stonemason was recorded as living on a Vienna farm. The census indicated he was born in Italy, despite his decidedly Anglo-American name of Michael Ferguson. That was the full extent of Italian immigration, three isolated individuals in northeastern Ohio in 1870. Yet within three years, the situation would change dramatically, and that transformation would be shaped by the rapid growth of the area's coal industry.

Since the ancestors of most local Italian Americans immigrated during the great wave that occurred between 1880 and 1924, little written history exists about the first arrivals beyond a few names in an old obituary or a few brief mentions in the *Youngstown Vindicator.* Donna DeBlasio and Martha Pallante's Images of America: *Italians of Youngstown and the Greater Mahoning Valley* doesn't venture into the decade of the 1870s. Joseph Sacchini's compendium of biographical sketches, *The Italians of Youngstown and the Mahoning Valley, Ohio,* notes that Marco Antonelli, for example, arrived in 1873 to work in the Coalburg mines. Yet his volume omits the historic context that initially drew Italians to the Trumbull County coal camps.

Labor historian Herbert Gutman chronicled the 1874 miners' strike at the Armstrong shafts near Pittsburgh in his 1964 article "The Buena Vista Affair, 1874–1875." He stated, "The first widespread use of Italian laborers in the bituminous coal mines—as armed strikebreakers—took place in 1874 near Pittsburgh."[2] While one can quibble over the specificity of his use of the word "armed," it's notable that Gutman made no mention—despite the numerous national newspaper reports of the era—of the labor action that brought hundreds of Italian strikebreakers to the Mahoning Valley's bituminous coalfields more than a year earlier. Similarly, neither Warren Whatley's article "African American Strikebreaking from the Civil War to the New Deal" nor Ronald L. Lewis's *Black Coal Miners in America* records the use of black replacements in the 1873 strike.

These are significant omissions, since ample newspaper coverage indicates that early January 1873 was one of the first instances of blacks employed as strikebreaking miners. In his "Reconstruction in Ohio: Negroes in the Hocking Valley Coal Mines in 1873 and 1874," Gutman discussed the 1874 Hocking Valley incident, saying "it was the first time that so large a number of Negroes had been used to break a strike."[3] Regarding the introduction of African Americans in Youngstown during the 1873 walkout, he is silent. Charlotte Erickson's detailed work *American Industry and the European Immigrant: 1860–1885* makes fleeting mention of Italian strikebreakers in the Mahoning Valley in 1873. Priscilla Long's exhaustive study of the U.S.

coal industry, *Where the Sun Never Shines*, covers the recruitment of Italians to Buena Vista in 1874.[4] Referencing the Gutman piece on the 1874 strike, she also omits the earlier entry of Italian strikebreakers in Trumbull County.

Indeed, the 1873 Mahoning Valley strike has received only cursory mention in history texts. Its five-month duration was briefly attested in *Youngstown, Past and Present*.[5] Beyond the abundant newspaper accounts of the era, one of the few substantial book references to the 1873 strike appears in Andrew Roy's volume *A History of the Coal Miners of the United States from the Development of the Mines to the Close of the Anthracite Strike of 1902*.[6] The Liberty Township author and Ohio chief inspector of mines may have witnessed the turbulent reception of the Italians at Church Hill and the aftermath of the camp riot where miners savagely assaulted them in reprisal for their participation as strikebreakers.[7] We hope that the research we offer here will reveal details that underlay the 1873 birth of the Mahoning Valley's Italian community. We also intend to correct more than a hundred years of misinformation and legend concerning its origins. Our analysis of the flawed dating in several publications appears in Appendix 1.

Before the unveiling begins, the authors would like to clarify several terms frequently used in the narrative. The first of these is **immigration**, found as "emigration" in nineteenth-century documents. There was a significant uptick in the numbers of Italians disembarking at U.S. ports beginning in 1870. Most immigrants in this study entered New York City at Castle Garden, a receiving facility especially built for foreigners arriving by ship. It opened in August 1855 at the southern tip of Manhattan Island. Ellis Island would open thirty-seven years later. Prior to 1875, the federal government did not regulate immigration to the United States. If one could survive the Atlantic voyage to America—no small achievement considering the perils—and answer a few oral questions, one could walk off the ship and into New York City unimpeded.

The Mahoning Valley, for the purposes of our study, includes the contiguous Mahoning, Trumbull and Columbiana Counties in Ohio. It is synonymous with the greater Youngstown-Warren metropolitan area.

Under the charge that trade unions were a constraint on trade, **union** membership could lead to arrests and fines. Despite the antagonism, unionized mine workers achieved a measure of power in the workplace, though legislative reforms and health and safety protections proved more difficult to win. The American Miners' Association (AMA) was formed in 1861 to create the first national coal miners' union. Wages, benefits and lobbying for mine regulation headed the agenda of the new organization.

Castle Garden around 1890. *Library of Congress Prints and Photographs Division.*

The AMA existed as a regional force in the Midwest, with active chapters in the Mahoning, Tuscarawas and Hocking Valleys.[8] By 1869, internal dissension had rendered the association powerless. Unlike the Workingmen's Benevolent Association, a union of predominantly anthracite miners, the AMA was a craft organization interested in representing miners, not other laborers found at a typical coal pit. During the Coal War of 1873, David Owens led the miners in the Youngstown area. It wasn't until October 1873 that another attempt to form a national trade union organization took flight: the Miners' National Association.

Strike, the withholding of labor by workers, had a different context in the nineteenth century, given that labor unions were extralegal. Until the passage of the National Labor Relations Act (NLRA) in 1935, there was no federal legislation protecting the right of workers to strike or to engage in collective bargaining with an employer. In the early 1870s coalfields of northeast Ohio and northwest Pennsylvania, local union leaders responded to grievances by calling a walkout and stationing demonstrators at struck mines, while operators marshalled law enforcement officers to keep worksites open. The press closely followed labor. Newspaper reports engaged the entire community and even the nation. In many cases, articles in nineteenth-century national and local journals constitute the only records available on the occurrences of strikes.

The authors use the language of **war** to describe the depth and scope of the hostilities between coal operators and miners. The 1873 strike covered a wide expanse of terrain in at least three counties, with a series of violent actions reported in Liberty and Hubbard Townships. Battle plans included marshaling several deployments—really companies of hundreds of men, some armed by their employers—brought in from afar and bivouacked to defeat the strikers. Miners mounted incendiary counterattacks that destroyed property owned by coal companies. As in war, serious injuries occurred, even death. Collaterally, the coal war in the Mahoning Valley immediately affected coal supplies for civilians and for industries in the Great Lakes region and had national repercussions. Out-of-state and local newspapers closely followed events, with almost daily coverage of coal operators' maneuvers, economic impacts or the plight of the strikers. The term "coal war" befits this narrative.

ACKNOWLEDGEMENTS

We gratefully acknowledge the advice, assistance and support of the following individuals and institutions: Stacey Adger, Anne DeSantis, Ed Bell, Gavin Esposito, Marcello Galasso, Ramón García-Castro, Donna DeBlasio, Steve DeFrange, William Farragher, Joyce Friddle, Enrico Grammaroli, Ann Harris, Priscilla Hayes, Joe Jordan, Mary Ann Lark, Sam Stewart Lombardi, Albert Madeline Sr., Robert and Carole Madeline, Dave Madeline, Daniel Madeline Sr., Anthony Dion Mitzel, Sam Orlando, Salvatore Papale, Nancy Rasmussen, Paul J. Ricciuti, Felice Santilli, Mary Jo Suhrer, Patricia Takacs, Connie Tarr-Bostardi, Roslyn Torella, Jennifer Tucciarone, Mike Vance, Mary Weese, Beth Wehrmeister, Thomas Welsh, Elizabeth Wrona, the America-Italy Society of Philadelphia, Google Books, Google News, the *Hubbard Soaring Eagle*, *La Gazzetta Italiana Newspaper*, Angela Marshall at the Lepper Library, Tim Monroe at the Liberty Township Administration Building, the Library of Congress's Chronicling America: Historic American Newspapers, the Lisbon Area Historical Society, Logan County Historical Society, the Mahoning Valley Historical Society, the reference staff at the Warren Library, the Public Library of Youngstown and Mahoning Valley, the Youngstown Historical Center of Industry and Labor and the *Youngstown Vindicator*.

The authors wish to acknowledge the support of GenealogyBank for the use of its material in our narrative. GenealogyBank.com is a leading online genealogical resource from NewsBank Inc., all rights reserved.

PART ONE: WAR

Foreigners who never saw a coal mine are imported, and for what?

—*"The Italian Miners"*
Indianapolis Sentinel, *October 1, 1874*

1

INTRODUCTION

FROM FIELDS AND PASTURES TO COAL CAMPS

The Pennsylvanian Period begins northeast Ohio's coal history. About 320 million years ago, forests of ferns and horsetails filled the steamy, tropical swamps. Primitive reptiles enjoyed their morning bask in the sun. Lush vegetation grew in the primordial soil where an Ohio coal camp would one day appear. Layer upon layer of decaying matter fell unnoticed to the ancient forest floor. These strata, in turn, were buried under tons of sediment. The weight of the overlying material hardened the dead plants into solid rock. The bands of organic debris were compressed into seams of coal. Not surprisingly, the period is also known as the Great Coal Age. This is the foundation of Ohio's mineral wealth. In the 1800s, directed now by human hands, the black deposits would spark another pivotal age, one of iron and steel.

Coalburg is an unincorporated tract in northwestern Hubbard Township.[9] Never a city, a town or a village, the settlement included its only official station, a post office. This was closed in 1913, when the dwindling population could no longer support it. For much of the last two hundred years, Coalburg has remained largely rural. In the 1850s, before it received its name, sturdy settlers of Irish, English and German descent farmed the place. Men like Stephen Doughton, Solomon Everett, Hugh Love, Isaac Price, James Burnett and Alexander Jewell tilled the land. In time, these fields would likely be passed on to their children. A rural way of life seemed destined to continue uninterrupted in this quiet little community.

In neighboring Mahoning County, John Webb edited a small newspaper called the *Canfield Sentinel*. In March 1857, an unusual story caught his attention. The remains of an ancient creature had been unearthed on a farm in Hubbard Township. The area was not known as a source of primeval relics, yet a team of men had excavated a six-pound tooth "of huge antiquity" there.[10] Sensing a good story, Webb dispatched a reporter to the site, a field owned by Hugh Love. Intrigued by the find, Webb published an article about the fossil in his newspaper. Word of his story reached Alphonso Hart and James Somerville, the editors of the *Portage Sentinel*, in Ravenna, Ohio. They reprinted Webb's fascinating account. The find was accidental, for the men were not searching for fossils. They were opening a coal mine. The news prompted great speculation, and the district was soon given the fitting name of Coalburg. The exceptional quality of the coal earned it the title "second to none."[11] The discovery paved the way for the rapid development of the area and for the arrival of the first Italians to settle in Hubbard Township and the Mahoning Valley.

Liberty Township, roughly five miles southwest of Coalburg and four miles north of Youngstown, offered another bounty of local coal. The first mine opened in 1862 on the Dennison Farm.[12] Next, the small farming community of Church Hill, in the same township, saw a rush of speculation when rich deposits were discovered under Dr. Robert H. Walker's cattle pastures.[13] Soon, nearly every homestead in the area was drilled. When the seams were mapped, it was declared that Church Hill encompassed the largest reserves in Trumbull County.[14] Its coal was regarded as some of the finest that was shipped to Cleveland.[15]

During its ascendancy, William Ritezel composed many articles about the busy little village. The editor and publisher of the *Warren Western Reserve Chronicle*, he proclaimed, "The Southern portion of Trumbull county is one of the richest coal sections in the State of Ohio."[16] At the heart of this bountiful territory lay Church Hill.

On June 3, 1868, the secretary of the state of Ohio granted a certificate of incorporation to the Church Hill Coal Company "for the purpose of mining stone, coal, ore and other minerals."[17] The partners in the new firm were Charles Arms, Evan Morris, John Tod, John Stambaugh Jr. and Jacob Stambaugh. The company extended rail lines to the shafts, installed heavy machinery and quickly erected modest lodgings for new workers. By the end of 1868, a hundred tons of fine block coal were hauled out of the

A farm in Liberty Township near the Church Hill coal mines, 1874. *Niles Historical Society.*

Church Hill mines every day. Their yield was expected to triple within a few years.[18]

By the middle of the 1870s, hundreds of men were digging beneath Church Hill's cornfields, where peak production reached more than five hundred tons of coal per day. The Centennial Shaft, known for its excellent coal, eventually employed 342 men. Only one other mine in the state boasted a larger workforce.[19] Within a decade, the leaders of the Church Hill Coal Company had transformed the sleepy hamlet into a bustling engine of commerce.

Since wealth creation and conflict play an important part in this story, at this early point it is important to recall the natural advantages that the Mahoning Valley possessed, for they underlay the great fortunes that were created here and the strife that erupted in the second half of the nineteenth century. In fact, the discoveries in the natural environment would position the valley to become an international industrial powerhouse. These included the iron ore that was easily accessible along the banks of the Mahoning River and the Yellow Creek near Struthers, a village five miles southeast of Youngstown.

Dug from the river sediments, the yellow ore was transformed into iron at James and Daniel Heaton's Hopewell Furnace, built around 1803. This was the first ironworks west of the Appalachian Mountains. The local limestone was another bounty from nature. Crushed into powder, it was added at the top of the blast furnace stack and served to remove impurities from the iron. Early quarries—in Lowellville, Mount Nebo in Struthers and Poland—made limestone an easily accessible commodity via the Mahoning River.

Coals suitable for use in furnaces are of two varieties; anthracite and bituminous. The former, commonly called "hard coal," has a higher energy content because of relatively few impurities. In contrast, bituminous, or "soft coal," is less pure and burns at lower temperatures. This dirtier coal was abundant in western Pennsylvania and eastern Ohio. But Mahoning Valley coal banks contained a mineral that was of exceptionally high quality: it was soft but burned hard.

This highly prized local resource went under several names: Sharon coal, Sharon no. 1, Brier Hill coal, Brier Hill block and Mahoning block. In *Iron Valley: The Transformation of the Iron Industry in Ohio's Mahoning Valley, 1802–1913*, Clayton J. Ruminski mentions that the Ohio Geological Survey classified the mineral as "No. 1 coal" and that it ran in veins "underneath Youngstown, Austintown, Boardman, and Poland in Mahoning County, and beneath Hubbard, Brookfield, Liberty, Vienna, and Weathersfield in Trumbull County."[20] In Youngstown, it was also found in Brier Hill. In Trumbull County, a seam of this mineral was abundant in Coalburg and Church Hill. As early as 1828, it was being mined at Mount Nebo, in Struthers.[21] In the 1840s, future Ohio governor David Tod began developing mines at Brier Hill. Within a few years, his superlative coal found markets beyond the Mahoning Valley. "Most of the citizens of Cleveland are acquainted with the 'Briar Hill' coal, which is considered the best and commands the highest price of any in the Cleveland market." By 1851, shipments of Tod's product were already reaching Chicago.[22]

During the local bituminous "coal rush" in the second half of the nineteenth century, the black mineral attracted buyers from rapidly developing industrial centers in the Upper Midwest. Early ironworks had relied almost entirely on charcoal as a fuel. Mahoning Valley coal powered the iron industry in communities along the Mahoning River beginning in the 1840s and, soon afterward, in the Great Lakes region as a growing export. By the end of 1872, over 1,500 tons of "black diamonds" were shipped out of the Youngstown area every day.[23] The following year, the valley achieved its maximum output, reaching a million tons for the first time.[24]

Navigable from Newton Township through Youngstown and beyond, the Mahoning River provided a commercial advantage. Then, with the completion of the Pennsylvania & Ohio Canal in 1839, new markets opened for the young industries of the Mahoning Valley. Youngstown and nearby villages no longer produced solely for the local economy, for markets in Cleveland and Pittsburgh could now be reached by canal. Products carried by waterways and, eventually, by rail would position the area for a century of growth in heavy industry with the world as buyer.

DAWN OF A NEW IRON AGE

While the first iron works had used hardwoods for fuel, by the 1840s, foundry and mill owners fired their furnaces using coal from nearby Trumbull County, which boasted the richest coalfields west of the Appalachians. Some of the most productive mines were in Coalburg. As one historian noted, this hamlet "in the southeast corner of Trumbull County, furnished one of the first iron-making coals to be used anywhere. This was the Sharon coal. It could be used without first being coked and it gave the Youngstown area an early impetus in the iron industry."[25] Another observed that, "Of the 11 or 12 local coals found in the Mahoning Valley it is only the Sharon coal that maintains the quality and thickness needed for mining."[26] Sharon coal fueled two early iron facilities, one in Youngstown and the other in Lowellville.

On January 27, 1846, a fledgling ironworks on the Mahoning River was granted a certificate of incorporation by the Ohio state legislature.[27] Among the several founders of the venture were Isaac Powers and the Wicks: Caleb B., Henry Jr., Hugh B. and Paul, all men who would thrust Youngstown onto the national scene as a powerful industrial center. Their pioneering firm, the Youngstown Iron Company, was soon producing a respectable four tons of finished iron every day.[28] After a few years of operation, the facility was shut down. In March 1855, Brown, Bonnell and Company purchased the business, promptly renaming it the Mahoning Iron Works. In later years, it would become the Republic Iron and Steel Company.

Around the same time, John Wilkeson, of Wilkeson, Wilkes and Company, built the Mahoning Furnace in Lowellville. This ironworks, originally called "Anna" and later renamed "Mary," was the first furnace in Ohio designed to use the Brier Hill (Sharon) coal in its raw, uncoked state.[29] In fact, Wilkeson's firm was the first in the United States to accomplish this feat.[30] The furnace

Mary furnace, Sharon Steel Hoop Company (Lowellville, Ohio). *American Iron and Steel Institute, Hagley Museum and Library.*

was blown in on August 8, 1846, by John Crowther.[31] The Crawford brothers purchased Wilkeson's operation about 1847, adding it to their mining and manufacturing empire. Already successful as coal men, they saw the investment in iron as a means of building wealth. The abundance of local, high-quality coal and the success of the Youngstown Iron Company and the Mahoning Furnace encouraged other manufacturers to build coal-powered furnaces in the Mahoning Valley.

2

THE COAL BARONS AND THE ARRIVAL OF THE RAILROADS

By the early 1860s, Coalburg's pastures and cropland had grown into a major Ohio coal camp that fed the area's growing industrial powerhouse. Almost overnight, a generation of subsistence farmers became wealthy businessmen. Lands once furrowed by plows were now gouged by pickaxes and rocked by dynamite explosions. Former cornfields, now coalfields, yielded a bounty of hundreds of tons of coal every day.[32] The coal rush was on.

Consequently, Coalburg became the scene of a frenzied real estate boom driven by coal. In November 1862, the Cleveland & Mahoning Railroad Company announced the "construction of a branch railroad from Youngstown to the coal-fields of Hubbard township, Trumbull County. The road will be about six miles and a half in length, and will terminate for the present on the land of Alex. M. Jewell."[33]

Not coincidentally, Jewell's farm lay at the edge of the rich Coalburg mines. Between November 1862 and July 1863, the railroad company purchased dozens of farms for its new track bed. On August 8, 1863, the first load of coal was shipped down the new rail line, which was christened the "Hubbard Branch."[34]

Madison Powers epitomized the new breed of men who were transforming the mineral-laden county. A successful cattle rancher and the owner of a thousand acres in Liberty and Hubbard Townships, he possessed a calculating eye for commodities other than livestock. Foreseeing the increasing value of coal, Madison purchased the Coalburg property of Solomon and Susan

Everett on August 11, 1862, paying the unheard-of sum of $10,000 for what had been marginal cropland. He opened his namesake shaft on the lot and soon leased its management to the Mahoning Coal Company. The pit later became known as Mahoning Mine 3. The purchase allowed him to amass a fortune of well over $100,000 by the time of his death.[35]

Iron and coal men from Youngstown—Chauncey Andrews, William Bonnell, William Powers and others—were also acquiring Coalburg properties. Alexander Jewell, Cornelius Price and Robert Porterfield made fortunes by leasing their mineral-rich lands to these entrepreneurs. However, among the Coalburg men, few were as successful as Stephen Doughton.

THE DOUGHTONS

Metals and coal marked the interests of the enterprising Doughton family. Stephen A. Doughton and his wife, Margaret Farren, lived in Valley Forge, Pennsylvania, where Doughton labored as an iron worker: "He was employed, during the Revolutionary War, at making arms for Washington's troops."[36] When the couple settled in Ohio in 1804, Doughton promptly built a small foundry in Niles, which was one of the first ironworks in Trumbull County. Stephen and Margaret Doughton homesteaded land on the western edge of Hubbard Township, still an untamed frontier. As a late-nineteenth-century atlas of the region noted, "at that time the almost trackless wilderness was inhabited by wild beasts and the more savage Indian."[37] Doughton often walked from his home to his ironworks in Niles, returning in the evening with wild game for dinner.

Stephen Doughton II, the namesake of his grandfather, was born in Hubbard Township in 1822. One early historian indicated that Doughton was a renaissance man who authored "several treatises on the money question, which indicate an unusual grasp of the subject."[38] The same source noted that he "wrote for his own enjoyment, rather than for remuneration" and was regarded "as a broad scholar and a deep critic." His self-taught background in economics would, no doubt, prove useful in the coming coal boom.

Stephen's interests included politics, and he served as "a candidate for the State senate and at one time [was] nominated for lieutenant governor of Ohio."[39] He was a country squire, managing "a four-hundred-acre farm which he scientifically and successfully conducted. When the Erie and Lake

Shore railroads built their lines close to the Doughton farms, each named a station in his honor."[40]

Above all else, Stephen Doughton was an entrepreneur. He established the coke furnaces at Washingtonville, Ohio, and was one of the founders of the Iron Works in Leetonia. When coal was discovered on his land, he was quick to capitalize on it, becoming "one of the pioneers in the coal business in Trumbull County."[41] Historian Joseph G. Butler Jr. noted that Doughton "exploited a number of coal fields, finding and testing out new fields, and after proving their value leased them for operation to practical miners."[42]

On May 18, 1860, Stephen Doughton leased his coal-rich land to William Powers and Joseph Brown. The property under consideration was Stephen's North Farm, covering most of Great Lot 22 in Hubbard Township. Although Doughton received just $1 in the transaction, he was promised 12½¢ for every ton of coal taken from his acreage. In addition, Powers and Brown agreed to rent the land for as much as $500 per year.[43]

A railroad was laid across Doughton's farm. Twenty-two acres of land lay between the rail line and the eastern edge of his estate. This wedge-shaped lot housed miners and served as the headquarters for Brown's operation. The parcel was named the Mahoning Coal Railroad Company's Addition to Coalburg. The miners called it the "Blocks," after the type of coal they found there. Within a few years, the place received a third name: "Little Italy."

CHAUNCEY ANDREWS, THE COAL KING OF YOUNGSTOWN

Nobody was more instrumental in spurring the development of Youngstown as an industrial and financial powerhouse than Chauncey Humason Andrews. Among his many endeavors, he founded banks, constructed railroads, built iron foundries and established a local newspaper, but he is best known as an early investor in coal mines.

Andrews was born in Vienna, Trumbull County, on December 2, 1823. The family moved to Youngstown in 1842, where his father opened the Mansion House Hotel. In later years, Chauncey assumed the management of his father's business. During this time, young Andrews developed an interest in coal speculation. Embarked upon a new career as a coal prospector, he sank his first shaft at Four Mile Run near Weathersfield in

Chauncey Andrews around 1880. *Harriet Taylor Upton and Harry Gardner Cutler,* History of the Western Reserve, Vol. 3 *(Chicago: Lewis Publ., 1910), University of Michigan.*

1853. The venture was a dismal failure. Four years passed before Andrews made his first major strike, on the Baldwin farm in Thorn Hill, where he eventually unearthed five hundred thousand tons of coal. Flushed with success, in 1858, Chauncey founded the firm of Andrews & Hitchcock, which operated coal mines and erected iron foundries throughout the Youngstown area.

By the outbreak of the Civil War, Andrews had established a mineral empire, transporting local coal from his Cleveland dock to ports throughout the Great Lakes. He became known as the "great coal king" of the Mahoning Valley.[44] Indeed, one nineteenth-century historian stated, "The extraordinary prosperity of Youngstown is due to Chauncey Andrews more than to all other causes combined."[45]

As a buyer or leaser, Andrews invested in many coal-bearing properties in Hubbard Township, which possessed some of the finest coalfields in the Mahoning Valley. One of these was the Burnett Bank, which he opened in 1862. It was a large railroad slope that over a twenty-year period produced as much as 450 tons of coal per day, much of which was sent to furnaces as far away as Chicago.[46] Six years later, he opened the highly productive Stewart mine in Coalburg, which he leased to the Mahoning

Coal Company. By 1868, Andrews & Hitchcock was the largest producer of coal in the state of Ohio.[47]

To facilitate the transport of coal from his mines, Andrews built the Hubbard Branch of the Cleveland & Mahoning Railroad. Beginning in 1863, coal arrived at Great Lakes ports over this line.[48] In 1869, Andrews personally managed the construction of the Niles & New Lisbon Railroad.[49] Jay Gould, the well-known New York railroad magnate, was associated with Andrews in this project. With the new line attracting the attention of investors from Europe, Andrews sold it to James McHenry & Company of London, who in turn leased it to the Atlantic & Great Western Railway Company. Ten years later, Andrews established the Pittsburgh, Youngstown & Chicago Railroad in conjunction with several notables, one of whom was William McKinley, the future president of the United States.[50] With the opening of the Niles & New Lisbon Railroad, Chauncey Andrews could now economically ship coal from his mines in Columbiana County. In 1870, he and his brother Wallace formed the New Lisbon Coal Company for that purpose.[51]

An important player in the coal business, Andrews was also a major force in developing the Lake Superior ore industry. He was a principal stockholder of the Kimberley Iron Company, which consisted of ten thousand acres of ore-bearing land in Marquette County, Michigan.[52]

In addition to starting industries, Andrews launched financial institutions in Youngstown. In 1880, he organized the Commercial National Bank of Youngstown and was vice president of the Second National Bank. He and former Ohio governor David Tod organized the Youngstown Savings and Loan Association, which later became the Mahoning National Bank. Although he never entered the political arena, Andrews was instrumental in designating Youngstown as the seat of government in the new county of Mahoning in 1873.

The glowing accolades heaped on him at the time of his death drew from his accomplishments as a shrewd businessman, developer of the valley's industrial infrastructure and philanthropist. The iron industry prospered during the Civil War, resulting in increasing demands for his coal. As the war intensified, coal prices rose, and Andrews's wealth increased. A Cleveland reporter questioned the coal baron's wartime profiteering: "How dare Andrews and Hitchcock attempt to ship a cargo of coal to Chicago."[53]

3

THE CIVIL WAR AND OHIO HEAVY INDUSTRY

For decades, the question of slavery had caused sharp sectional strife. On April 12, 1861, this tension erupted into war between the North and the South. The bloody conflict would accelerate the growth of Ohio's young industries. Already a growing manufacturing region before the Civil War, the North had an industrial capacity strengthened by the Union's demand for war supplies and for new railroads to transport provisions and troops. In fact, the North's advantage in heavy industry and rail construction, with significant concentrations of both in Ohio, proved a major factor in defeating the mostly agrarian South: "Like all other wars, the Civil War was a war of supplies even as much as a war of men. And Youngstown's little industries were not unimportant by any means. The close of the war in 1865 found them enlarged and active."[54]

While initially there were more foundries in southern Ohio, along the Ohio River, a trend was developing that would see the state's iron industry develop rapidly in Ohio's northeast quadrant. By 1870, Youngstown's population had almost doubled from the previous decade. The numbers in neighboring Hubbard Township more than tripled in the same period.[55] The foundries and forges fed by Sharon coal energized this growth spurt.

Offering passenger and freight service to almost every part of the country, Ohio boasted the greatest number of track miles in the nation. Therefore, in the summer of 1863, the Buckeye State's efficient rail lines were a seductive and logical target for Confederate brigadier general John Hunt Morgan's marauding forces. After the end of a month-long incursion through Tennessee, Kentucky and Indiana, Morgan's cavalry was poised to enter the state by crossing the Ohio River. Alarmed by the news of the approaching rebel raiders, Governor Tod ordered the state's militia to protect Ohio's southern counties. He exhorted the citizenry to "take their axes and obstruct the roads over which Morgan's troops would be compelled to pass."[56] Unfortunately, the governor's order failed to reach most of the militia units in time. On July 13, Morgan crossed into Ohio, penetrating north of Cincinnati. Unimpeded, the Confederate forces destroyed bridges and rail lines, going on to loot government supplies and civilian warehouses. News of the invasion spread panic throughout southern Ohio. Working their way through the Hanging Rock area, Morgan's raiders then headed northeast in an apparent move toward the Mahoning Valley.[57]

A young Joseph G. Butler Jr.—residing in Niles, close to the Confederate incursion into Columbiana County—assessed the peril this way:

> *One Sunday in mid-summer, when the weather was extremely warm, a horseman rode into Niles with the news that Morgan had crossed into Columbiana County and was headed north, of course directly for Niles. It was generally believed that he meant to raid the Mahoning Valley, destroy the iron mills and capture the money in the banks. The money was not such a great amount, perhaps, but the iron mills were of immense value to the government, as from them and from the blast furnaces came a great deal of material needed to win the war.*[58]

Underlining Butler's concern, Clayton J. Ruminski writes:

> *One of the Mahoning Valley's most notable furnaces used to make pig iron for rail production was Alexander Crawford's Mahoning furnace in Lowellville. Morgan's raid supposedly targeted the Mahoning furnace, which would have cut off Crawford's raw pig iron source used to manufacture rails at his rolling mill in New Castle. Union forces captured Morgan's remaining cavalry at Salineville in southern Columbiana County, only thirty-three miles south of Lowellville, leaving the Mahoning furnace, as well as the valley's industrial infrastructure, intact.*[59]

The Civil War was a national tragedy, but it was a boon to Youngstown's iron and coal industries. By the end of the conflict, over a dozen new blast furnaces had opened in the city and the adjoining communities. The amount of iron ore transported to the foundries in the Mahoning Valley rose

THE CHRONICLE.

WARREN, O.

WEDNESDAY, JUNE 27, 1866.

WILLIAM RITEZEL, Editor and Publisher.

The Mineral Railroad Co.

NOTICE.—The undersigned, Corporators of the above Company, recently authorized by letters of incorporation, to carry into effect the power granted to construct a railroad in Hubbard, Trumbull County, Ohio, give notice that books will be opened for receiving subscriptions to the Capital Stock of said Company, at 12 o'clock, noon, on the 7th day of July, at the Hotel of Nathaniel Mitchell, in said Hubbard.

WM. BONNELL,
WM. R. BURNETT,
A. K. PRICE,
J. G. BUTLER, Jr.,
RICH'D BROWN.

June 6 1866 5w

Left: Formation of the Mineral Railroad Company. *From the Warren Western Reserve Chronicle, June 27, 1866, Chronicling America, the Library of Congress.*

Below: Stock certificate from the Mahoning Coal Railroad Company, 1880s. *Unbekannte Autoren und Grafiker; Scan vom EDHAC e.V.*

dramatically, from 3,000 tons in 1863 to over 90,000 tons in 1864.[60] The quantity of coal exported from the Mahoning Valley mines to markets in Cleveland grew from 100,000 tons in 1854 to 278,000 tons in 1864.[61]

By the end of the Civil War, the Mahoning Iron Works was manufacturing more than sixty tons of hardware each day in the form of railroad spikes, nails, bars, hoops and sheets of iron. Brown, Bonnell & Company had transformed the small riverside foundry into "the largest mill west of Pittsburgh."[62] In later years, the enterprise became the largest iron manufacturer in the United States.[63] It owned the furnaces and the mines. However, it didn't own the roads between them, and the railroad companies levied high tolls on coal shipments to Youngstown.

Determined to minimize transportation costs, the owners of the Mahoning Iron Works decided to build a railroad from their mines to their mill. On May 18, 1866, William Bonnell, William Burnett, A.K. Price, Joseph G. Butler Jr. and Richard Brown announced the formation of a new enterprise, the Mineral Railroad Company. Prospective investors were invited to gather at Nathaniel Mitchell's hotel in Hubbard on July 7, 1866. The books would be opened for subscriptions to the capital stock of the new company.

This venture led to the birth of the Mahoning Coal Railroad Company on February 25, 1871. William Bonnell, Joseph H. Brown, Richard Brown, Augustus B. Cornell and David Himrod served as the partners in the new corporation. Their goal, the construction of a seven-mile track from Youngstown to Coalburg, would guarantee a steady supply of cheap fuel for their furnaces. The newly laid tracks lowered shipping costs and swelled profits. By 1872, their assets were valued at $1.5 million,[64] clear evidence that coal barons and miners were creating enormous wealth.

4

FROM ITALY TO CASTLE GARDEN, NEW YORK CITY

A NEW ECONOMY AND THE EXODUS OF ITALIAN LABOR TO THE UNITED STATES

The closing months of 1872 saw a dramatic increase in emigration from Italy, a reality that had roots in the end of feudalism and, most immediately, in the abusive practices of certain steamship lines. The freeing of the serfs was a societal earthquake that detached peasants from their bonds to the land, their centuries-old source of survival. Occurring almost sixty years prior to the political unification of the peninsula, the French occupation of Italy under Napoleon Bonaparte was the principal catalyst of this dramatic shift from a feudal to a market economy.

From 1799 until 1815, a series of French client states and kingdoms imported many of the projects of the French Revolution into other parts of Europe: legal reform, the sale of church and nobles' lands, religious and intellectual freedom, separation of church and state and the promotion of science and industry. To achieve the goal of creating a market economy, authorities in these satellite states put ecclesiastical and baronial property up for sale, while converting town and village commons into real estate.[65] The moves had the potential of creating a new class of land-holding small farmers, but in Italy, they resulted in enriching a new order of local elites, land speculators and absentee landlords. Peasants, who had little capital to purchase plots and who for hundreds of years had possessed rights to farm and graze livestock on village-owned commons, found themselves without a way to feed their families. The Kingdom of Italy was born in 1861, the same year Giuseppe Garibaldi's victory over the Bourbons delivered the defeated Kingdom of the Two Sicilies to Victor Emmanuel II, united Italy's first modern monarch. The new government, whose leadership was incubated in the northern Piedmont region, soon embarked on an ambitious program to raise revenues with the goal of creating a modern, liberal state that continued the market economy introduced earlier by the French occupation. The largely rural country faced several severe problems in this shift, not least of which were a weak agricultural sector and lack of manufacturing. Additionally, by the second half of the nineteenth century, an expanding birth rate was outstripping the country's ability to gainfully employ its workforce.[66] The widespread areas that produced cereals were especially marked by an underemployed, seasonal labor force.[67] Once the grain harvest was finished, there was very little opportunity for work elsewhere.

Hopes were high for progress in the former Bourbon kingdom, where centuries of backwardness and traditionalism prevailed. This southern area, often called the Mezzogiorno, had just sixty miles of railroads in 1860.[68] Ninety percent of its towns were unconnected by roads. Furthermore, the southern provinces were populated with dispossessed peasants turned bandits who menaced public order. To counter the highwaymen, the new government unleashed a reign of terror in the countryside, where martial law was declared. Dennis Smith remarks, "There were 120,000 soldiers concentrated in Sicily and the South, almost half the national army."[69] Despite expectations that the new government would bring changes, progress was elusive, and as the political errors of the new, northern-led regime mounted, southern Italy suffered an economic crisis.

Luigi Campanelli, longtime mayor of Capracotta in the then-Abruzzi-Molise, produced a history of his region in which he listed denunciations of the early central government. He inveighed against Italy's political leaders, who increased taxes, imposed new fees on the sheepherding industry, increased Italy's debt, exacerbated the problem of the brigands and levied a tax on gristmills—effectively hiking the price of bread.[70] Consequently, in the 1870s, a lack of steady work, crushing taxation and rents and brigandage that produced a repressive police response compelled many southerners to join Italians from other regions who were leaving for Northern Europe and the Americas. Previous immigration from Italy to the United States had been negligible. Only 924 migrants were counted in 1865. The tally rose to 2,891 in 1870, but the increase wasn't uniform, and it was followed by a temporary decline that persisted through the fall of 1872.[71] However, the downward trend was abruptly reversed on November 8, 1872, when 266 Italian immigrants arrived on the steamship *Denmark*. Ten days later, twice as many disembarked from the *Holland*.[72] More ships followed as an unprecedented surge of Italians began crowding the nation's ports. During the first ten months of the year, an average of seven Italians entered the United States every day. In the final eight weeks of the year, the daily rate skyrocketed to nearly forty.[73] But unlike well-to-do tourists on holiday, most of these wanderers bore the scars of financial deprivation. For decades, they had endured worsening economic conditions that drove many to the brink of poverty. Most of them clung tenaciously to their ancestral homeland until an unexpected catalyst triggered their sudden departure. Penniless and landless Italians began pouring into the United States.[74] The Castle Garden station in the Port of New York bore the brunt of this influx. Remarkably, many of the Italians comprising this tidal wave came from a small part of the then province of Campobasso encompassing the village of Carovilli and the town of Agnone.

Today, Agnone lies in the province of Isernia, within the region known as the Molise. It was one of the fifty-six royal towns under the Bourbon kings, and by the nineteenth century, its cultural achievements had earned it the title *l'Atene del Sannio*, the "Athens of Samnium."[75]

Filippo Carosella, Filippo Marcovecchio and Alfonso Saulino, along with wife Angela Maria, were peasants in Agnone. Carosella and Marcovecchio were *contadini*, or farmers, while Saulino was a shoemaker. For them and most of southern Italy's peasants, especially those in Agnone, the post-Unification years brought hardship.

As an agriculture settlement, the *comune* or town of Agnone has faced challenges related to topography and elevation, a feature of its location in the southern Apennines. William A. Douglass describes the climate in two-thirds of the town's area as "unpredictable" or worse for Mediterranean agriculture.[76] The impact of the free market reforms begun by the French and continued by the Kingdom of Italy's modernizing program made life for peasants such as these four *Agnonesi*[77] even more difficult. Traditional agricultural lands fell into the new, competitive real estate market where only the wealthier townsmen, the *galantuomini* in Douglass's study, had cash to participate.[78] From 1815 to 1845, the number of families owning land in Agnone fell by about 50 percent.[79] Agrarian reform at the end of feudalism did award plots to peasants, but these parcels proved too small to sustain a family.

In the fall of 1872, the four Agnonesi must have taken notice of exuberant characters who were beginning to appear in the towns of southern Italy. The hucksters, likely in the pay of steamship companies,[80] posted circulars

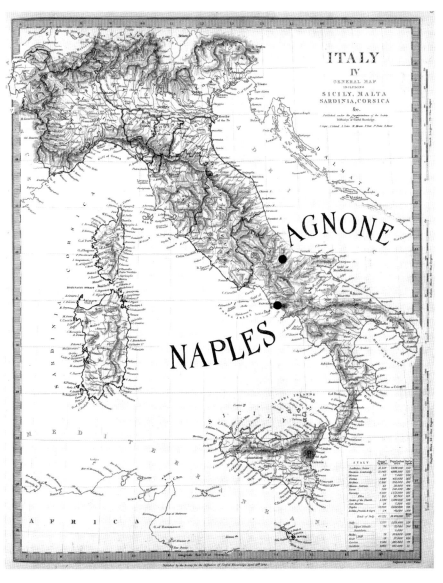

Italy, prior to Unification, modified to show Naples and Agnone. *David Rumsey Map Collection, www.davidrumsey.com.*

advertising the fortunes that immigrants could make in America.[81] Immigration officers in the United States were aware of these parasites and their scams. Many Italians, unfortunately, were not: "They showed us all maps of America and told us all about the country. 'You get rich there very fast,' they said, 'and no one works very hard. It is a fine country, you should sell everything, even your wife, and go there.' "[82] One impressive stranger's description survives in detail:

> *He had been in America, and wore fine clothes. The people of the district had never seen so grand a personage. He said he was very poor when he left Italy, and all one had to do was to go to America and come back rich. He was going to America to get more money, and had only returned to tell all his countrymen that they might secure some of the gold that could be dug out of the ground in that rich land.*[83]

Rochas & Figlio of Turin operated a shipping agency engaged in loan fraud and misinformation. An advertisement for its services appeared in the *Gazzetta della Provincia di Molise* on December 1, 1872. The agents of the Rochas firm lured villagers with tales of the good life in America. The final advertisement for the agency was printed in the *Gazzetta* on December 8; two weeks later, the paper published an article condemning the Rochas scam and warning prospective emigrants of the company's deceptive practices.[84]

Impacted by the post-Unification upheavals, Filippo Carosella, Filippo Marcovecchio and Alfonso Saulino decided to immigrate to America.[85] Their wives stayed behind except for Angela Maria, who accompanied husband Alfonso. Leaving Agnone, they made their way to Naples, more than a hundred kilometers away. From there, they journeyed by boat to Marseille and then by train to Le Havre, where they would take a ship headed to America. On December 10, 1872, they boarded the SS *Erin*.

In the early 1870s, routine passenger service from Italy to the United States was practically nonexistent. Instead, Italian emigrants bound for America took a less direct but more reliable route through the seaports of Northern Europe. Travelers who undertook this circuitous passage were known as "transmigrants." Most southern Italians heading to the United States followed a similar path to the Agnonesi. The first stage in their journey was a trek from their homes to Naples, with the poorest among them arriving on foot.[86]

Residents from other parts of Europe journeyed by rail, or other primitive means, to ports like Bremen or Rotterdam, where they could

Rochas steamship advertisement.
From Gazzetta della Provincia di Molise, *December 1, 1872, Biblioteca Provinciale "P. Albino" Campobasso.*

take "feeder ships" to England. Between 1836 and 1914, almost 20 percent of all European emigrants passed through the British ports of Liverpool, Southampton, London and Glasgow on their way to America.[87] Many travelers took advantage of these affordable and competitive routes years before direct passage was commonly available from ports in Southern Europe. Many would fall victim to abusive steamship lines.

FROM LE HAVRE TO AMERICA
ON BOARD THE SS *ERIN*

First class cost a thousand lire,
Second, a hundred,
Third class, pain, death,
And the stench of sweat from the hold,
And air fouled by stagnant water.

—*"Titanic," Francesco De Gregori*
Translated by Ben Lariccia

The National Steam Navigation Company, also known as the National Line, was a British firm operating a fleet of transatlantic steamers. One of these was the *Erin*, a four-thousand-ton, coal-powered ship outfitted with three masts and a single funnel. By 1872, the *Erin* was making regular trips between London and New York. On December 5 of that year, fifty passengers boarded it at the Victoria Docks in East London. Among them was Joseph P. McDonnell, a reporter for the *New York Herald*. He had been assigned to investigate steamers leaving Liverpool. When he heard how poorly the National Line treated its steerage passengers, he reserved a berth on the *Erin*. No sooner had the steamship raised anchor when the first sign of trouble appeared. Upon passing Gravesend at the mouth of the Thames, McDonnell noted there were no sailors at the lifeboats.

Already five days behind schedule, the *Erin* crossed the English Channel and docked at Le Havre, where over 700 additional passengers embarked, 549 of whom were Italian emigrants.[88] Those from Agnone included Filippo Carosella, Filippo Marcovecchio and the Saulinos.[89]

Upon reaching Le Havre, all but three of the stewards abandoned the ship. Its propeller was damaged and its boilers faulty. Understaffed and underpowered, the compromised vessel departed for America. Plagued by stormy weather, the fifteen-day crossing became a twenty-eight-day nightmare during which the ship barely reached a speed of five miles per hour.

Steamship *Erin*. © *National Maritime Museum, Greenwich, London*.

McDonnell recorded the plight of the unfortunate Italians. Against regulations, three hundred of them were lodged in makeshift bunks lashed to the main deck in front of the toilets. They spent most of the trip huddled together, shivering and drenched with seawater. The quality of the food was no better than that of the bedding. The bread was fair, but the meat was hard and stale. The tea and coffee were never hot, and the stench of the soup was unbearable. The potatoes were tasteless, "black and soft as wet soap." At mealtime, three stewards attempted to do the work normally performed by a dozen. As they were often drunk, the result was utter chaos. The foreign passengers were mocked, cursed and struck with food. Some of the passengers were seriously injured by the blows and needed medical attention. The captain was required to inspect the ship twice each day from stem to stern and maintain the discipline of his crew. He did so only three times during the long voyage.[90]

McDonnell's appalling account reveals how the inhuman conditions took their final, terrible toll. Six people died during the crossing from lack of medical care, all of whom were Italian emigrants. One of those was an infant who was born at sea. Immediately after its birth, the child was taken from its mother and "handed over to the steward, who fed it three or four times during the night with a spoon as large as a ladle. Shortly afterwards the child was returned to its mother and expired."[91]

As the ship approached New York, the temporary bunks on the deck were torn down to allow the vessel to pass inspection. For the last days of the voyage, the three hundred passengers who had been berthed in these crude arrangements were forced to sleep in the open on the bare, wooden deck. The *Erin* limped into New York harbor on January 1, 1873. As a contemporary news account observed: "The Italian emigrants who arrived from Havre in the *Erin* looked wretched. They were much emaciated, and bore the traces of the rough weather and the ill treatment received on board."[92]

For the weary passengers, the terrible ordeal at sea was finally over. Regarding the Italians, a reporter for the *New York Herald* lamented "they were victimized in their own country before they left it; they were victimized at their starting and during every stage of their journey to this country, and they were victimized by their loudest-voiced friends on their arrival."[93] To use an apt nineteenth-century phrase, the Italians arrived in the United States as "pauper labor," indebted, easily exploited and less free than their American counterparts.

After the four Agnone travelers passed inspection at the Castle Garden facility, they joined thousands of other immigrants who had entered the

United States through the Port of New York. Many Italians seeking the company of their fellow countrymen went to the Five Points district in Manhattan. Some of them joined a growing colony there that became known as "Little Italy." The "Bend," on Mulberry Street, was at the heart of this community. It was also the center of an overcrowded, crime-infested slum.

Teams of unemployed and destitute Italians, often under the supervision of labor contractors, took jobs in New York City's public works, which included the street-cleaning department. Captain Thomas Thorne, the head of the division, hired several hundred Italians to shovel snow in January 1873. The press, curious about the newcomers, asked if he was satisfied with their performance.

> *He says that they are a most excellent class of working men, able-bodied, diligent, faithful, polite, orderly, and exceedingly honest. He has never had to deal with laboring people with whom he has been better satisfied. In his opinion, we are to have a very large immigration from Italy of this class, and he regards their coming as a great benefit to the country.*[94]

However, many immigrants didn't fare so well. That same month, the *New York Sun* gave a different assessment of the Italians' circumstances:

> *Six hundred Italian emigrants are now in this city destitute. They came to our shores filled with bright ideas of the New World, and expected to find work ready for them as soon as they landed. Their little stock of money has been expended, and they begin to feel the pangs of hunger. They are sober and able-bodied, bear testimonials from the Italian Government of industry, and seem willing to work at any price. They have been accustomed to farm, railroad, and mining works and are willing to go wherever they can gain a living. It would be a charitable act to give employment to these poor strangers, and those who wish to secure cheap and efficient labor could apply nowhere to better advantage.*[95]

Some Americans were moved to pity at the sight of the poor immigrants; others were filled with contempt. The *New Orleans Republican* gave an exceptionally discouraging report on the growing numbers of Italians entering New York:

46

Nearly a thousand more of the unwelcome Italian immigrants have arrived at this port within the last week—the steamship Denmark, which came in on Saturday evening, having landed a fresh consignment of two hundred. The whole number of this class who have arrived here during the past six weeks is about three thousand, of whom but a small proportion have been able to find employment, or finding it, have proved themselves capable. Temporary occupation has been given to a considerable number by the street cleaning bureau, in the removal of snow from the streets, but there is little else for them to do, and they are still a charge upon the city. The three ship loads who arrived last week are lodged and fed at our public institutions, and if this sort of work is to go on, it seems to be but fair that other cities should share with New York the pleasures of compulsory charity. Our people are willing to bear a share of such burdens, but they cannot see why the Italian shipping agents should be permitted to make our port the sole destination of thousands of paupers.[96]

Unemployed, sick or destitute immigrants were quartered at the State Emigrant Refuge on Ward's Island. Located eight miles from Castle Garden on the East River, the agency was operated by the Commissioners of Emigration. Also home to an insane asylum, the building formed part of the largest hospital complex in the world. Immigrants who couldn't find jobs were given temporary housing there.

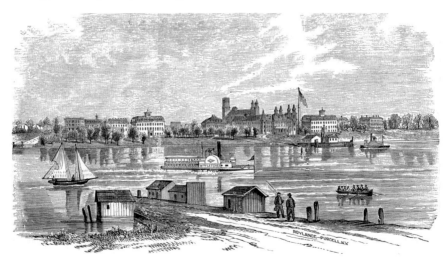

"Front View of the State Emigrant Refuge and Hospital Institutions, Ward's Island," 1861–80. *New York Public Library.*

In October 1867, the Commissioners of Emigration opened a labor exchange at Castle Garden where prospective employers could hire workers free of charge. The exchange was equipped with a telegraph, enabling managers anywhere in the country to monitor the immigrant labor pool.[97] The service revolutionized the process by which employers located prospective employees. In the next decade, the Mahoning Coal Company would take advantage of the rapid communication with Castle Garden. The result would alter the fortunes of immigrants and of American miners in the Mahoning Valley.

5

OF MINES AND MINERS

Down in a coal mine, underneath the ground
Where a gleam of sunshine never can be found
Digging dusty diamonds all the season round
Down in the coal mine, underneath the ground

—From "Down in a Coal Mine"
Louie Hooper and Lucy White, performers, Cecil Sharp, collector
September 1903

Each dawn as I rise, Lord,
I know all too well
I face only one thing:
A pit filled with hell.

When the Great Seal is broken
The pages will tell
That I've already spent
My time in hell.

—From "A Coal Miner's Prayer"
Brenda Graham

INSIDE A MINER'S HEAD

William Ritezel remarked on November 28, 1866, in his newspaper, the *Warren Western Reserve Chronicle*, about the coal miners of Hubbard Township: "Some of them are very respectable, quiet moral people, and make good citizens, but many of them need, as in the language of our parson, the Rev. R.W. Crane, a 'good threshing in the name of the Lord.' "

The coal miner was a special breed of man. Impulsive, capricious and rowdy to a fault, he was also independent, tough and fearless. He knew a mine could instantly become a tomb. "He may be crushed to death at any time by the falling roof, burned to death by the exploding of gas, or blown to pieces by a premature blast. In no part of the country will you find so many crippled boys and broken down men. Not many old men are found in the mines."[98]

If a miner survived the dangers and emerged in the evening unhurt, he had good reason to raise a little hell: "The miners were a hard drinking lot as a rule, and on payday went out to celebrate, so that the first part of the week following payday, there were many absent from work. The operators tried staggering paydays, but it did little good."[99]

Miners occupied a unique place in the nineteenth-century American workforce. At this time, they were paid by the ton, not the hour. They owned their tools,[100] set hours and controlled many aspects of work underground in the absence of foremen. A common saying of the era was "a miner is his own boss."[101] It was often noted that a miner developed a strong attachment to his mine, almost a proprietary one.[102] While some were given to excessive drinking, many miners were pillars of their community and could be found holding elective office, heading congregations and even serving on boards of education.

David Owens was a hardscrabble miner from Wales. He arrived in the Mahoning Valley in the 1850s and labored in various coal banks in the Youngstown area. In 1871, he was elected president of the local miners' union, where he repeatedly called for the establishment of regulations for the ventilation of mines. He also worked to mediate disputes between the union members and the operators. In November 1879, Ohio governor Richard Bishop appointed him state inspector of mines. Owens was described as "a practical miner" who was highly regarded by his constituents, unlike his predecessor, "a politician who never saw the inside of a mine."[103]

Despite their difficult lives, some miners became valued citizens in their communities. Many attained the status of heroes as first responders in life-threatening situations far underground. In a crisis, there was no one more knowledgeable about mine rescue than a miner.

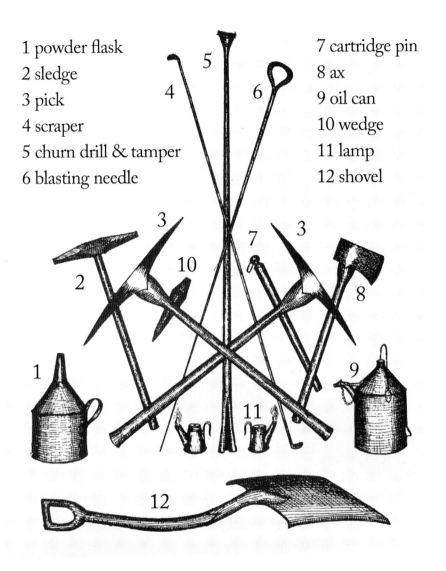

1 powder flask
2 sledge
3 pick
4 scraper
5 churn drill & tamper
6 blasting needle

7 cartridge pin
8 ax
9 oil can
10 wedge
11 lamp
12 shovel

Sketch of miners' tools. *Andrew Roy*, A History of the Coal Miners of the United States from the Development of the Mines to the Close of the Anthracite Strike of 1902 *(Columbus: J.L. Trauger, 1907), University of Michigan.*

BURIED ALIVE IN A COALBURG MINE

The critical role miners played in deep-pit rescue operations was underscored by the events of Friday, July 21, 1865. On that day, John Turrill, Thomas Bowen, Jacob Miller and Thomas Miller reported for work as usual at a Coalburg bank owned by Madison Powers. Accompanied by Jacob's dog, they entered the shaft at two o'clock in the afternoon. They would not emerge for almost a week.

The entrance to the Powers mine was located near Yankee Creek, a stream whose waters were held in check by a small dam. The flow was usually reduced to a trickle in the summer, but the third week of July in 1865 had been an unusually wet one. Heavy thunderstorms caused the water to rise. At nine o'clock on the evening of July 21, a terrific downpour unleashed a torrent, collapsing the dam and flooding the entrance to the mine. A boy was working at the entrance of the shaft that evening driving a team of mules. When the water began rushing in, he cut the ropes to free the mules and raised the alarm. Miners hurried to the scene and frantically tried to stop the flow of water. Word spread quickly that four men were trapped underground.[104] A thousand mining men across the Mahoning Valley threw down their tools and ran to the flooded mine to join the rescue effort. Across the state line in Pennsylvania, colliers in the Shenango Valley dropped their picks and hurried to the scene of the disaster. Men from twenty-five mines gathered in Coalburg to help their imperiled comrades.[105]

Working through the night, the rescuers were finally able to stop the flood. At daybreak on Saturday, workmen began drilling into the hill above the highest point in the mine, hoping the men would be there. A crowd of two thousand people gathered at the site; among them were the terrified wives and children of the four trapped men.

Bowen, Turrill and the Miller brothers were working a half-mile from the mouth of the shaft and were completely unaware of the dangerous situation. While "they smoked their pipes" and "cracked their jokes,"[106] the water crept soundlessly up the slope toward their chamber. At four o'clock in the morning, Bowen and Turrill started down the tunnel to go home. Stunned at the sight of the seething dark water, they went back up the slope to the highest gallery they could find. They watched with terror as the water rose up to their necks. With their escape cut off, all they could do was wait for rescue or death. A grim demise from slow starvation wasn't the only threat in that chamber; a pack of rats was also imprisoned in the pits.[107]

SATURDAY, AUGUST 5, 1865.

THE HUBBARD COAL BANK ACCIDENT.

Details of the Rescue of the Imprisoned Miners.

Entrapment and rescue of coal miners. *From the* Cleveland Leader, August 5, 1865, *Chronicling America, the Library of Congress.*

At noon on Sunday, the drill had cut through sixty-eight feet of rock and reached the interior of the mine. The rescuers called into the shaft, but there was no answer. An anxious twenty-four hours passed while a vigil was kept at the hole. The next day, a voice from deep below broke the silence. It was Turrill and Bowen; they were alive and asking for food. Immediately, crackers were lowered into the hole, but hungry rats devoured them before they reached the miners. Bottles of soup and whiskey were lowered to the entombed men: "One of the imprisoned men cried up through the drill hole to 'send down more whiskey.' This message from the tomb produced a roar of laughter, as it was well known that he who sent it was partial to the flowing bowl."[108] The prisoners told how they had heard the drill and struggled through the darkness to reach the source of the sound. When the drill broke through, so much water poured down the hole that they plugged it, fearing they would drown. When the water stopped, they opened the hole and called up to the surface.

At the flooded entrance to the mine, pumps were throwing out streams of water, and two lines of men bailed it out of the hole, passing buckets up the hillside. A corps of Youngstown women, who had set up cooking stalls in the field, worked day and night to feed the mass of volunteers.[109] As food continued to reach them and their rescue seemed imminent, Turrill and Bowen became cheerful and even joked about their predicament. By Wednesday afternoon, the water level was low enough for the rescuers to enter the tunnel. Wading through chest-high water, they found Turrill and Bowen at the drill hole. The exhausted duo could barely speak when they were reunited with their families at the surface. The rescue team returned to the watery depths to search for the Millers. They had been missing for five days, and there was no sign they were still alive.

The area where the Millers were working was in a different part of the mine, and the entrance was completely submerged. At eleven o'clock on Wednesday night, the rescuers had all but given up hope when a train arrived from Youngstown bringing more men. Henry Burnett, the co-conductor of the Hubbard Branch railroad, vowed to find the Millers "dead or alive."[110] With a small boat in tow, they once again descended into the flooded pit. At a narrow passage far underground, the situation looked so hopeless that all but two of the company abandoned the rescue attempt. The remaining two men, tied with a rope, pushed resolutely forward. They finally reached a small chamber where they were greeted by the frenzied barking of Jacob Miller's dog.[111] Jacob and Thomas Miller were also there, leaning against the wall in a murky pool, numb and unable to speak. "Afraid to expose them too suddenly to the fresh air, they were placed in the boat, taken to a higher room, wrapped in blankets, and retained there for about an hour, when they were brought out after being in that terrible room five days and six nights."[112] The boat carrying the men emerged from the shaft at dawn on Thursday morning.

As soon as they were able to speak, the Millers recounted their harrowing experience. On the night of the storm, water surged into their small workplace. The dark flood rose within three inches of the ceiling, "compelling them to throw their heads back to keep their faces out of water."[113] Propped against the wall and leaning on each other, they took turns sleeping fitfully. As the tide slowly fell, they were finally able to sit, shivering and exhausted. Weakened by hunger and exposure to the cold, they gradually lost consciousness, though still accompanied by their vigilant canine companion. When the search party finally gained access to the chamber, they were dragged by the alert dog to the senseless miners. Against all odds, heroic miners had averted a disaster in Coalburg's dark underbelly.[114]

ANDREW ROY, A POWERFUL VOICE FOR MINERS

The incident in Coalburg and other disasters, such as the Avondale mining catastrophe of September 6, 1869, stunned the nation's mining camps.[115] It was obvious to many in the collieries that the lack of adequate regulation caused many preventable accidents. Casualties in Ohio mines resulted in 700 injuries and 250 deaths in 1873.[116] Among the voices raised for the safety of Ohio miners, none was more influential than that of Andrew Roy, a Scottish immigrant and miner who settled in the coal community of Church Hill. Poor ventilation and the lack of escape shafts were ever present threats in the nation's mines, dangerous conditions that continued for decades despite the toll they took on miners' lives.

Andrew Roy around 1907. *From A History of the Coal Miners, University of Michigan.*

Roy emerged from the Chartist movement in the United Kingdom, which pressed for the elimination of political corruption and the expansion of voting and other rights for the working class. As the united voice of millions of ordinary Britons pushed for reforms to improve the workplace, 1863 saw the organization of the Miners Association of Great Britain to advance these aims in the collieries.[117] Miners who left the United Kingdom to settle in the United States carried the ideals of Charterism and workers' rights to the coal communities of their adopted land.

While much coal mining in the Mahoning Valley occurred on or near the surface, there also existed mines that ran deep underground. In this latter case, miners complained bitterly about the lack of proper ventilation, adequate drainage and multiple escape shafts. In addition to the struggle to secure fair wages, the movement to organize miners took up the issue of safety regulations as part of the battle with operators. Roy lent his energies to the campaign to secure safe working conditions for the state's coal diggers.

A decade of toil in the mines of Trumbull County had acquainted Roy with the hazards of unregulated mining. Seeking a public forum to aggressively promote the issue of improving miners' safety, he joined forces with Alonzo Fassett, the pro-labor editor of a Hubbard newspaper, the *Miners' Journal.* Using the pen name of Jock Pittbreeks, Roy authored a series of articles in 1868 and 1869 urging the Ohio legislature to establish safety regulations in the mines.[118] On September 17, 1870, miners convened in Church Hill to discuss "the question of mining, and making laws for the regulation and ventilation of coal mines, and for the protection of the health and lives of miners."[119] On November 5, 1870, a resolution to draft such a law was added to the agenda of a miners' convention held in Youngstown, where it won the unanimous approval of the membership.[120] The proposal was presented to the Ohio General Assembly in February 1871.

Coal operators sped to the legislature in Columbus to lobby against the proposed bill. On March 20, 1871, miners responded with a mass meeting and demonstration in Youngstown. From their place of assembly, three thousand miners descended on the city's center.[121] American flags, a brass band and banners bearing the slogans "United we stand, divided we fall" and "In union there is strength" animated the crowd. All were united in backing the reform measure. Later, Roy and John B. Lewis, with the meeting's resolutions in hand, took off for the state legislature.[122] Youngstown had served as the venue for miners' agitation; the city would soon play that role again.

The miners' bill was defeated at the end of the legislative session in April. More action was plainly needed. With support from local union leaders and political allies, the emigrant from Scotland won legislation to enact reform. On May 2, 1871, in a concession to years of organizing by Roy and the miners, Ohio governor Rutherford B. Hayes announced the establishment of the Ohio Mining Commission.

The following year, the legislature passed an act regulating the workings of the mines, but it was powerless, since not a single coal operator adhered to its provisions. Finally, after years of organizing by Roy and the miners, meaningful reform passed in the Ohio General Assembly in 1874. Entitled an "Act to Regulate Mines and Mining,"[123] the comprehensive law was designed to rein in the free-wheeling mining industry. Its first provision established the office of a state inspector who would oversee all mining operations in Ohio. On April 1, 1874, Governor William Allen appointed Andrew Roy as the first chief inspector of mines.

6

THE COAL MINERS' STRIKE OF 1873

Which side are you on?
Which side are you on?
My daddy was a miner and I'm a miner's son
And I'll stick with the union 'til every battle's done

—*"Which Side Are You On?"*
Florence Reece

KING COAL

As the 1860s ended, Trumbull County coal production grew. In 1867, the county's mines yielded over seven million bushels of coal, far more than that from any other county in the state of Ohio. In that year, more than a fifth of Ohio's total production of coal came from the Trumbull County mines.[124]

> *The coal field of Trumbull county is mainly confined to the five southeastern townships, viz., Hubbard, Brookfield, Liberty, Vienna and Weathersfield. They constitute the most important, and in every way characteristic of the block coal fields of the State. For many years they produced more coal and better, not only than any other equal area in Ohio, but they placed Trumbull far in the lead of the coal-producing counties.[125]*

In 1867, over a thousand tons of coal were dug out of the mines in Hubbard Township every day.[126] The enormous quantities of the "dusty diamonds" found in the prosperous coal camps of Hubbard and Coalburg produced visible signs of wealth. Banks and retail establishments grew to meet the spurt in population. On May 26, 1869, William Ritezel reported in the *Warren Western Reserve Chronicle*:

> *We made a few hours visit in Hubbard, last Wednesday, and were surprised to see the evidence of business and prosperity that have sprung up all over the town, from center to circumference, since our visit a few years since. The census of 1870 will probably show a greater than five-fold increase in the population of Hubbard during the last decade. Coal is king in the Mahoning Valley.*

Six months later, Ritezel wrote about Coalburg, once a crossroads in Hubbard Township but now boasting banks, saloons, passenger and freight rail service and growing retail outlets.

> *Things are going off in a very business-like way, in this little village. The banks in the vicinity are daily responding to the miner's pick, and sending out their treasures. The neighing of the iron horse is heard several times a day, and its groanings too, as it bears away its goodly burden of fine, black coal.*[127]

Ritezel continued his tour of Trumbull County, visiting the booming mines of Church Hill. On January 5, 1870, he wrote in the *Warren Western Reserve Chronicle*:

> *We are blessed with reliable deposits of mineral, that is daily being removed to the various markets, from which production large amounts of money are returned and distributed through the numerous channels of business....The energetic Church Hill Coal Co., are now mining three hundred and fifty tons per day, and are employing about one hundred and eighty men.*

America's hunger for finished iron continued to rise in the years following the Civil War. Spurred by this growth, the coal market also grew, and Ohio miners demanded a share of the rising profits. In May 1872, their pay was raised from eighty cents to a dollar for every ton of coal they mined. In November of the same year, workers pressing for higher wages initiated isolated strikes in parts of Ohio and Pennsylvania. Operators in the Mahoning Valley quickly submitted to the clamor and raised workers' pay by ten cents per ton of coal.[128] But their timing was poor, and a rumor circulated the raise would soon be retracted.[129] By autumn, pig iron prices had dropped from fifty-five to forty dollars a ton.[130] Calls for iron slumped, and as inventories rose, the iron makers issued fewer orders for coal. Faced with a declining market, mine owners from the Shenango and Mahoning Valleys met at the Tod House in Youngstown to discuss their options. On December 20, 1872, they unanimously agreed to cut the price they paid to their workers by twenty cents per ton effective January 1, 1873.[131] Their decision was certain to precipitate a strike. The Church Hill miners were the first who refused to accept the cut; they walked off the job on the first day of the new year. Miners in other villages soon followed, and within a few weeks, most of the mines in the Mahoning Valley were idle.

"A DISASTROUS STRIKE"

In addition to stopping the flow of coal, the miners' walkout brought iron production to a standstill. Dwindling coal reserves caused furnaces to shut down, adding more men to the unemployment rolls. As soon as the Mahoning workers quit their coal banks on New Year's Day 1873, the miners in Ohio's Tuscarawas Valley, fifty miles from Youngstown, joined them. In 1872, the colliers of the Mahoning and Tuscarawas Valleys determined to coordinate their efforts in order to secure greater control over wages. Solidarity between miners at the two locations proved to be key.

Earlier, at Cleveland on November 4 of the previous year, the Tuscarawas Valley coal mining association had resolved that the price paid to Tuscarawas miners would correspond to the amount received by their peers in the Mahoning Valley.[132] Each time the Youngstown men secured a raise, their counterparts in the Tuscarawas sector vied for an increase. But the Cleveland accord was more like a guideline than a rule, since the operators weren't bound to it. For example, their proposed wage reduction didn't extend to the Tuscarawas hands.[133] Even so, the miners in the Tuscarawas Valley rallied to join the walkout of their pick-and-shovel comrades in the Youngstown coalfields. Their maneuver was intended "to help their brethren of the Mahoning valley"[134] by creating a scarcity of coal in the region, thereby forcing the Youngstown area operators to the bargaining table.[135]

New-York Tribune.

NEW-YORK. FRIDAY, FEBRUARY 7, 1873.

DISASTROUS STRIKES AMONG COAL MINERS. YOUNGSTOWN, Ohio, Feb. 6.—It is estimated that nearly 7,500 coal miners are now on a strike in this neighborhood and the Tuscarawas Valley. Many strikers have large families, who are suffering for the necessaries of life. A number of the iron workmen have been compelled to suspend operations for want of coal, thus swelling the army of unemployed laborers. Three hundred colored miners have been brought from Virginia to work in the Bowers Coal Mine, and the experiment has proved so successful that other mining companies are contemplating the importation of colored laborers. There seems no probability of an early settlement of the question between the striking miners and their employers, and business is almost at a stand-still.

Beginning of the coal miners' strike of 1873. *From the* New York Tribune, *February 7, 1873, Chronicling America, the Library of Congress.*

Strikes among the Ohio Coal Miners, Wadsworth, O., Jan. 24

They are having some queer times among the mines up here in the Mahoning, Shenango and Tuscarawas Valleys. To-day, the miners…are all "on the strike." Meeting an old miner at Wadsworth yesterday, I asked him what was the trouble. "The trouble!" he repeated—"why, they want to crush us out—the bosses do…we're backed up agin 'em, and we will kill every miner who don't go with us." And he slammed his begrimed old hand down on an empty beer barrel.[136]

THE COAL OPERATORS' VALUABLE WEAPON

OUTSOURCING, A NEW WAY TO DEAL WITH LABOR

As miners' strikes and union organizing increased during the Civil War, especially under the leadership of the American Miners' Association, newspapers reported on rumors of coal operators who were considering employing replacement workers from outside the community. In the Brady's Bend coal strike of 1864, three hundred Belgian immigrants found employment as strikebreakers near Pittsburgh.[137] Six years later, in the Ohio camps near Niles[138] and Nelsonville,[139] rumors circulated that Chinese labor was being sought to run the struck coal pits there. On July 27, 1870, mine owners met in Akron to discuss the use of Chinese immigrants in their mines.[140] Frustrated owners from the Tuscarawas Valley met the same day in Akron and resolved to hire foreign laborers to end a walkout in their pits. The strikers took the threat to heart and returned to work, now earning fifteen cents less per ton than before their strike.[141] The importation of Asian laborers never materialized. Yet an 1871 strike in Vienna, eight miles northwest of Youngstown, prompted mine owners to hire seven German immigrants. The effort failed when the fresh recruits met opposition from the miners.

The striking miners notified the newcomers that their presence was not agreeable, and that if they persisted in working, the consequences to them would probably be damaging to life and limb. For some time the German miners have been escorted back and forward from their work by persons interested in their safety.[142]

While this early attempt failed to introduce immigrant labor to defeat an Ohio coal strike, some in the business community were following the successful introduction of low-cost, exploitable labor in other parts of the country. Outsourcing was in the wind, and it didn't favor coal diggers.

ARRIVAL OF AFRICAN AMERICAN STRIKEBREAKERS IN YOUNGSTOWN

White man, don't be scared—forty nine more just 'hind me

—*"Here Me Comes"*
Ohio Patriot, *January 10, 1873*

The industrial empire of Chauncey Andrews owed its existence to his exceptionally sharp and calculating business sense. Closely monitoring the coal markets in the fall of 1872, he decided that miners' wages must be cut to balance a decrease in the demand for coal. As the leader of Ohio's coal operators, he called the owners' meeting of December 20, where he dictated the reduction. Anticipating a strike, he recruited mercenaries and mustered his troops before the first shot was fired. In the coming war with the miners, he developed a novel stratagem for a decisive win. Weeks before the pay cut was announced, he engaged the services of John P. Justis, an employment agent in Richmond, Virginia. On December 13, 1872, Justis ran the first in a series of advertisements in the *Daily Dispatch* recruiting African Americans to work in Andrews's New Lisbon mines. To sweeten the deal, Andrews promised free housing and coal for the personal use of his new hires. By the time his miners struck on January 1, he had already outflanked them with a detachment of black miners hired in Virginia. They arrived by train in New Lisbon on January 6: sixty-three men with their wives and children.[143] The townspeople did not interfere when the Virginia men entered the mines.[144]

The coal miners at New Lisbon, Ohio, struck for an advance of wages last Monday, and their demands not having been acceded to, have been unemployed ever since. On Tuesday last the proprietors introduced into the mines some sixty negroes, from Richmond and Norfolk, Va., for the purpose of supplying the places of those miners who refused to work at the old rates. The appearance of the newly-employed laborers caused considerable curiosity and excitement in town and at the mines. It seems that this is the first attempt that has been made to solve the difficulty of miners' strikes in this manner, and the result will be looked for with interest.[145]

On January 10, the *Ohio Patriot* ran a cruel, satirical piece with an accompanying racialized cartoon that left no doubt that the strikebreakers' race ought to be of keen interest to the newspaper's readership. Using a racial epithet, the mocking article proposed to warn the general public that the dusky pigmentation of the Virginia men would darken the landscape, causing New Lisbon's chickens to roost in broad daylight.[146]

The strategy of rapidly importing replacement workers achieved so much success that it was quickly implemented in neighboring facilities. When news spread that the Tuscarawas operators were arranging to fill their abandoned shafts with blacks from Virginia, the striking miners protested. "They think the negro is good enough in his place in the South, but they do not want him among them."[147] William Powers, another New Lisbon mine owner, adopted Andrews's plan. Powers's advertisement, published on February 1, 1873, in the *Daily Dispatch*, called for "one hundred white and colored laborers."

Five days later, a train pulled into the Youngstown depot carrying more than a hundred African Americans from Virginia.[148] "Headed by an old slave driver,"[149] they were immediately brought to the Powers Coal Bank in New Lisbon. Apparently, no whites were among them. The newcomers were baffled when they were handed guns in addition to pickaxes: "Apprehending that their lives might be threatened, or attempts made to intimidate them, they have been furnished with fire-arms, and as quite a number of them were soldiers, it is expected they will be able to take care of themselves."[150] Upon recruitment in Virginia, the men had not been told that they were going to be strikebreakers.

HERE ME COMES!

A white man burdened by the weight of a black man. *From the* Ohio Patriot, *January 10, 1873, Lepper Public Library.*

Richard Trevellick around 1895.
University of Michigan Library, Joseph A. Labadie Collection.

This wasn't the first or the last time mine owners hired unsuspecting replacements.

The recruitment of black miners from Virginia sparked an intense reaction among the citizens of Youngstown. James H. Odell, editor of the *Mahoning Vindicator*, ranted, "To import negroes or Chinese to fill the place of white laborers, if it can possibly be avoided, is a degrading and damnable outrage. Are we understood?"[151] On Saturday, February 15, 1873, an "indignation meeting" was organized to protest the coal operators' tactic.[152] Accompanied by colorful banners and blaring music, 2,500 striking miners marched through Youngstown.[153] The procession converged on Public Square, where John B. Lewis, president of the Grand Lodge of Ohio, addressed the demonstrators. Joining Lewis was Richard Trevellick, president of the National Labor Union (NLU), who had come from Detroit to attend the event.[154] That Trevellick appeared in Youngstown underlines one of labor's chief concerns in the post-slavery era: how to check the exploitation of black labor as a ready pool to use against union workers. As reported by the press, the purpose of his Youngstown appearance was "to remonstrate against the introduction of colored miners."[155] Ironically, a major goal of the NLU's National Labor Congress of 1869, during which Trevellick had been elected president, was the organization of a labor union for African Americans.[156]

As a precaution, Youngstown mayor John D. Raney ordered the closure of saloons during the event. The day passed without violence, but a strong racial animus permeated the gathering. The incendiary orators inflamed the audience, and it was feared that "after some fiery speeches, they were ready to rend the garments of the first unlucky nigger they saw."[157] As the February 26, 1873 *Warren Western Reserve Chronicle* reported, "Among the banners carried in the procession was one bearing this ancient device, once so familiar in Democratic mass meetings: 'Niggers are Free; We are Slaves.'"

Coal operators outside the Mahoning Valley had employed black scabs several times before Andrews introduced them to his New Lisbon mines. In February 1871, African Americans replaced striking miners in Mason

City, West Virginia, and a few months later, another group entered pits in Estill County, Kentucky, which had been idled by a stoppage.[158] In December 1872, a team of African Americans was hired at the North Shaft in Springfield, Illinois, when rank-and-file workers refused to work.[159] All of these were local incidents that passed virtually unnoticed, having been reported in but a handful of newspapers. The Virginia blacks who came to New Lisbon may have been the first group of African Americans to cross a picket line during a regional miners' walkout. As such, the importance of this event was raised to the first magnitude by newspapers from Boston to San Francisco and in dozens of other places in between. What was so riveting about the Mahoning Valley labor conflict? What could have thrust the controversy into the national spotlight? If they intended to demoralize white strikers, the coal operators had no better weapon in their arsenal than the black strikebreakers. Civil War veterans were numbered among the ranks of striking miners. The use of blacks to replace them, in a former free state, must have shocked the onetime Union soldiers. A Confederate general warned, "You northern people don't know what you have done. You will yet see these blacks you have freed go North and come into competition with free white labor."[160]

A VIRGINIA SOURCE FOR BLACK MINERS

If white replacements were so difficult to find, why were African American ones so easily found? The answer lies in the Confederate ruins of the Old South. Headquartered at 9 Fifteenth Street, in Richmond's former slave market with its not-yet-dusty auction houses of horror, the enterprise of John P. Justis, in 1872, was in many ways a budding type of the South reborn. He must have sensed the wide-ranging and palpable possibilities unleashed by the demise of chattel slavery, for the entrepreneur made a remarkable entry into the faraway Mahoning Valley market via his traffic in black working men.[161] Whereas the old auctioneers had profited from the sale of slave labor, Justis developed his forte in marketing wage labor.[162] A cursory review of his newspaper advertisements in the *Daily Dispatch* reveals a job agency that provided many freedmen with jobs.[163]

In the case of Chauncey Andrews's New Lisbon mines, the true nature of the Ohio employer's request for miners must at first have remained hidden to the job seekers. Initially, how could the African Americans who signed to work for the coal operator know that the goal of the trip north would be to deliver a cargo of black strikebreakers? The Justis ads were silent on that issue. As the cattle car of new black recruits neared the New Lisbon destination, it's quite likely that the train took on armed guards and that a contingent of local police met the suddenly aware replacement miners.[164]

What could have induced African American workers to respond to the call to work the Ohio coal mines? It's most likely that they were attracted by remuneration unavailable in the Richmond area. Or perhaps conditions in Virginia spurred them to investigate possible resettlement in Ohio. Despite the defeat of the Confederacy and the emancipation of slaves in the secessionist states, the hopes of newly freed Southern blacks met serious disappointment following the end of the Civil War. General Sherman's Special Field Order No. 15, signed by Secretary of War Edwin M. Stanton and promoted by several in the federal Freedmen's Bureau administration,[165] encouraged former slaves to expect a program of agrarian reform, one that would create a class of independent farmers homesteading on land they had once made productive as slaves. By April 1865, Union forces were in possession of almost a million acres of Confederate land.[166] But postwar interventions undermined and finally killed any promise of land distribution to the freedmen. An executive order by President Johnson in 1865 restored to planters all land seized by the Union army. Not much later, any idea of land redistribution as a policy within the Freedmen's Bureau soon became a virtual dead letter.

In January 1866, to underpin plantation agriculture and achieve control over recently freed people, the Virginia legislature enacted a vagrancy law. (In 1865 and 1866, states throughout the defeated Confederacy enacted a host of similarly repressive laws commonly known as the post–Civil War "black codes"—whites were exempted.) Among other provisions, the act bound blacks to farm labor through mandatory contracts. Freed slaves and even antebellum free blacks were caught up in the maws of this legislation. Those who could not produce a signed labor agreement were subject to arrest as vagrants. Sentenced, they were sent as convict labor and leased to work off their fines on plantations and in mines. The main effect of the legislation was to deny African Americans full freedom. Furthermore, the binding of emancipated black labor to agriculture via contract eventually evolved into the system of peonage known as sharecropping.

Beginning in 1868, Congress, led by the Republican Party, undertook the reconstruction of the former Confederate states in a program of legislative, economic and social reform backed by federal military occupation. Southern legislatures, now racially integrated for the first time and led by pro–civil rights Republicans, overturned the dreaded black codes. A period of advancement for blacks ensued in Richmond, where African American men served on city council.[167] But 1868 also marked the dawn of the Ku Klux Klan in Virginia, where the terrorist organization boldly published murderous threats against blacks and their Republican supporters in the *Enquirer & Examiner* and in the *Daily Dispatch*, Richmond dailies.[168]

Significantly, the first commercial production of coal in the American colonies occurred in Virginia, in the Richmond Basin, located fourteen miles from the city of the same name, where deposits of high value bituminous coal led to a thriving mining industry worked by free and enslaved blacks.[169] In the years prior to the Civil War, blacks often worked in these coalfields shoulder-to-shoulder with white miners.[170] After the war, labor agencies in Richmond actively sought blacks for mine work in and out of the South. One of these was the firm of Werth, Rathbun and Company. In November and December 1866, the agency advertised weekly in the *Daily Dispatch* soliciting "colored men who are expert miners" for hire at the Carbon Hill mines a few miles west of Richmond. A few years later, another Richmond bureau employed the same newspaper to enlist "One Hundred Good Colored Miners" to work in the Eureka mines near Chattanooga.[171] Likewise, in June 1872, J.P. Justis advertised for "One Hundred Colored Miners" to work in the coal mines of Jackson County, Illinois.[172]

In the neighboring state of Tennessee, the presence of blacks in the pits was not embraced. In the August 22, 1871 *Memphis Daily Appeal*, a journalist wrote "From the Coal Fields," noting a large influx of Welsh, English and Scottish immigrants who were settling in the Cumberland Mountains of eastern Tennessee. The author observed that the newcomers, mainly farmers and shepherds in their home countries, were vying for jobs in the local coal mines. Their avoidance of the indigenous blacks caught the attention of the reporter. "It is a curious fact that while all these Europeans were abolitionists, they have, in practical everyday life, an unconquerable aversion to negroes." The author remarked, "Negroes are not suffered to become miners. Wherever they have been employed the miners 'strike,' and negroes are not permitted to acquire the art of extracting coal from the pits."

These and other circumstances affecting the Southern black community in the postwar years could have influenced skilled freedmen and other black miners to cast their lots with Justis, a bet that took them all the way to the

New Lisbon mines of Ohio's Columbiana County,[173] where whites could not be induced in numbers adequate to break the 1873 miners' strike.

Why would Chauncey Andrews choose to incur the high costs of importing labor from afar to keep his New Lisbon mines open? This was a population of African American workers without connections to New Lisbon and without ties that could offer aid or comfort. In an area with extremely few blacks, the safety of the Virginia men would lie totally with the mine operator. In fact, at one coal camp, owners armed the African American strikebreakers to protect them from striking miners.[174] The large Youngstown demonstration against the arrival of black replacements considerably raised the possibility of racial violence.

William Powers followed the successful example of Chauncey Andrews and opted to employ black miners because, like Andrews, he could not attract local strikebreakers to defeat the 1873 strike. There is no evidence that either of the coal operators made a public appeal for white Mahoning County replacement workers. In a word, they were compelled to look far from Columbiana County for manpower in sufficient quantity to break the miners' walkout.

On February 17, 1873, six weeks after the start of the Mahoning Valley walkout, miners struck the Brazil works near Knighstville, Indiana. On March 10, 1873, J.P. Justis posted an advertisement in the Richmond *Daily Dispatch* seeking "colored miners" willing to work in the Indiana mines. He contracted fifty-two blacks and delivered them to representatives of the Brazil collieries, who had come to Richmond to obtain the men.

> *Colored Laborers Going West. Messrs. Thomas H. Watson, and M.D. Watson, representatives of the Indiana coal and iron company and Western iron company, Knightsville, Indiana, and Mr. John J. Schrack, agent of the Otter creek black coal company, Brazil, Indiana, are in the city, and will send west quite a number of colored men from the city and state to work in the mines and furnaces of the companies mentioned. The parties will be ticketed through by James L. Waldrop, esq., the energetic agent of the Baltimore and Ohio Railroad.[175]*

Upon arriving at the Brazil pits, some of the blacks refused to enter, stating, "that they were not apprised of the state of affairs before coming; that they were only told that there was plenty of work and good pay."[176] As in the Mahoning Valley situation, they hadn't been informed they were acting as armed strikebreakers. The newcomers had entered an arena occupied by twelve hundred angry strikers. Three weeks later, an angry mob descended on the mining camp and surrounded the barracks housing the blacks.[177] Although guarded by local police, the compound was besieged by nearly every resident of Knighstville. Rocks were thrown, shots were fired, and a guard was wounded. Governor Thomas Hendricks sent reinforcements to the encampment, and peace was restored.[178]

> *The riots at Knightsville, Indiana, in which a mob of striking coal miners, led on and incited to violence, it seems, by their wives and mothers, have been attacking a corps of colored miners who had been brought to supply their places, are in effect another serious defeat for the miners' unions, who have combined in an attempt to dictate what price shall be paid for mining coal throughout the Northern States. Without doubt there was in the attack something also of race prejudice—there are certain classes of foreigners who can never be at peace with the negroes.*[179]

About sixty miles southeast of Columbus, Ohio, lie the coalfields of the Hocking Valley. On April 1, 1874, nearly two thousand of the region's miners struck when operators demanded that coal should be quarried by the ton rather than the bushel.[180]

> *It is now known that the strike in the Hocking coal mines occurred at the instigation of the miners of the Mahoning Valley, to compel operators in Hocking coal to pay as high prices for coal in the cars as is paid in Mahoning Valley.*[181]

A month of negotiations between the miners and operators followed the stoppage, but every attempt to reach a compromise failed. In the midst of the impasse, Chicago businessman Minor T. Ames arrived in Columbus to deal with the walkout. Ames was the vice president of the Lick Run Coal Company, which operated mines in the Hocking Valley. He decided to end the standoff by hiring a black workforce from Virginia to replace the striking men. Ames contracted the services of J.P. Justis to supply the men.

On May 23, 1874, Justis posted an advertisement in the Richmond *Daily Dispatch* calling for "500 colored men, miners and laborers, to go near Columbus, Ohio, by the 1st of June." This was an enormous request, far larger than the numbers requisitioned by his Youngstown and Knightsville customers in the previous year. On June 11, a large force of blacks arrived in the Hocking Valley under cover of darkness. Although an exact head count was never made, Justis had succeeded in fulfilling his clients' needs. Estimates of the size of the detachment ranged from 340[182] to more than 800.[183] A squad of policemen accompanied the cohort to Nelsonville, where they were equipped with rifles and revolvers. "Some of these men are desperadoes, used to rough usage, and if they are molested there will be desperate work."[184]

Riders on horseback raced through the countryside, spreading news of the incursion. Soon, a long line of townspeople from nearby Carbondale paraded into town, accompanied by "a band of music and flying colors."[185] Joined by the strikers and a cadre of newspapermen, the throng surged toward the colliery of Thaddeus Longstreth, where the black conscripts were stationed. One newsman described his entry into the once-peaceful valley, which was rapidly being transformed into a theater of war.

> *Reaching the brow of a slight elevation we were surprised by the scene that burst upon our vision. On an open plateau, at the foot of a range of low, scraggy hills lay the encampment of the colored miners, who at this moment were industriously drilling, their brightly burnished muskets and bayonets glistening and glancing like silver in the last rays of the sun. They were divided into companies and squads, with regularly appointed officers, &c., and made a very good drill for the brief time they had been broken in. They had their pickets thrown out and admission within the encampment was not attainable without the countersign. However, our little reportorial force advanced until stopped by a bayoneted musket in the hands of a great gigantic black, who cried in a thunderous bass voice, "Halt! Who goes dar!" "A friend without the countersign," was the response from our party. "Advance, friend, and give an account of yourself." This was done with admirable expedition, our representative informing the ebony picket that we wished to see the proprietor of the mines, Mr. T. Longstreth, who was dispatched for and shortly appeared and gladly conducted us within the lines to headquarters, in a narrow ravine between the hills. The shades of evening were now fast enveloping the landscape, but we took a careful look through the camp. The negroes are great stalwart fellows, resolute and unflinching, and most of them old soldiers of the late rebellion, while a good portion of them are fresh from the Arkansas troubles and anxious for an encounter with the white strikers.[186]*

The union men, crouching behind their defensive line, taunted the blacks. John Putnam, Governor William Allen's secretary, arrived in Nelsonville that evening. After urging the strikers to refrain from violence, he crossed the barricade and entered the blacks' encampment. Thomas Reich, the president of the Nelsonville union, came to the Longstreth works and urged the blacks to lay down their arms and join the miners' union. After a score of black desertions, the alarmed operators managed to stop the exodus by urging the remainder to sing "Rally Round the Flag."[187] That night, a few shots were fired between the pickets, but no injuries were reported.[188] In the morning, the African American strikebreakers began working in the coal banks. The first carload of coal bound for Columbus was draped with an American flag.[189]

The families of the old miners suffered so much that many of the men wished to return to their jobs. But the union was adamant, insisting that none of their members would re-enter the mines. On June 24, striking miners captured three men who had returned to work. Ropes tied around their necks were thrown into a tree, and the captives were threatened with hanging.[190] An anonymous author wrote verses in defiance of the owners and their new recruits:

We Miners wanted nothing,
But what was honest and right;
The bosses wouldn't give in
But got the niggers for to fight.

They placed the muskets in their hands,
With powder and some ball;
To fire at the Union men,
If they did anything at all.

The Operators will not pay,
The fair and honest thing;
But turn against the Union men,
And fetch the niggers in.

For the darkies they have come sir,
And that you all do know;
To take the place of white men,
And him to overthrow.[191]

The walkout continued a few months longer, but the determination of the operators overcame the miners' resolve, and the walkout collapsed in failure.

The importation of black replacements was the decisive factor in the defeat of the white union miners of the Hocking Valley.

The Hocking Valley operators manipulated the African American volunteers, thrusting them against the anger of mostly Welsh strikers. The mine owners had cut their Gordian knot but in so doing opened a deep wound between white and African American miners. In Indiana and Ohio, African Americans found themselves suddenly constrained to play roles the coal operators had designed for them, that of strikebreakers. It wouldn't be the last time.

ARRIVAL OF THE FIRST ITALIAN REPLACEMENT MINERS

In the summer of 1870, a strike shut down operations in Stark County, not far from the Mahoning Valley. "The coal mine owners of this section have been endeavoring to obtain coal miners from Europe, through their agents in New York."[192] On September 9, 1870, fifty European immigrants arrived in Stark County, having been contracted by Morris Cohnert of New York. The enlistees were promised a dollar per ton of coal at a newly opened mine in Dennison, Ohio. Upon their arrival, the men found out that they would be strikebreakers earning only eighty cents per ton. They turned down the work, demanding either their pay or train fare back to New York.[193]

In February 1873, despite some difficulties, experiments with black replacement workers had reopened some of the Youngstown area mines. But on March 14, 1873, the *Ohio Patriot* reported that a demand for higher wages had swept the ranks of the black miners in New Lisbon. Very likely their rebellion shook the owners' confidence in depending on more imports of African Americans from Virginia. Rejecting the New Lisbon gambit, the owners of the Mahoning Coal Company decided to implement the battle plan of the Stark County operators three years previous. In that action, the mine owners had sidestepped American workers by enrolling migrant laborers far from the American mainstream. The enlistment of foreigners would constitute a novel ploy in the Mahoning Valley, one that would raise the intensity of the fight to a new level. This time, mine owners would hire not fifty, as in the Stark County case, but hundreds of immigrants, a great number of whom would be Italians.

In the middle of March, telegrams flew between Youngstown and New York. The coal operators needed men that the labor exchange had in droves.

The Italian immigrants on Ward's Island, who had so lately been liabilities, figured now as assets. The Mahoning Coal Company dispatched Mr. Sanford as its representative to the Castle Garden station, where he contracted more than a hundred men to work in the company's mines at Coalburg.

Filippo Carosella, Filippo Marcovecchio and Alfonso Saulino were among Sanford's recruits. They had survived the grueling voyage of the steamship *Erin* and the bitter winter in New York. Now, accompanied by Alfonso's wife, Angela Maria, the men from Agnone were embarking on the last stage of their exodus to America.

When Sanford negotiated the agreement with the Italians, he led them to believe they would be working in a new coal bank. He did not inform them they would be used to break a strike.[194] This deception was the common thread running through the recruitment pitch of the mine owners. It was first used on the "miners from Europe," then on the Virginia blacks and now on the Italians. Only later would the newcomers confront the unavoidable truth that they were replacing striking miners. But at the time, bound by contract, they had no alternative other than to proceed.

On March 19, the migrants arrived at the railroad station in Leavittsburg, a few miles north of Youngstown. When the train reached the station, "some of the miners came aboard and said there would be trouble, as there was a strike here."[195] Only one of the Italians understood English, but the meaning of the words and the belligerence in the miners' faces were unmistakable.[196] This was the first time the immigrants heard about the situation in which they were now embroiled. With a deep sense of foreboding, the anxious travelers continued their journey to Coalburg.

Incredibly, when the immigrants arrived in the coal camp, they were left alone and unprotected amid many angry men. At first, the uneasy immigrants and the grim onlookers eyed each other nervously. After a while, the strikers stepped forward, appealing to the Italians and offering them money to return to New York. Some of the immigrants agreed to leave and were given $342 for their expenses.[197] Those who remained received bloodcurdling threats from the miners, who drew fingers across their throats as a sign of warning. The terrified Italians promptly left Coalburg and walked through the night toward Youngstown. By morning, they had wandered into different parts of the city, frightened and friendless. Employees of the Mahoning Coal Company found fifty of them at the depot and persuaded them to return to Coalburg. The rest were taken in charge by Alonzo Fassett, the editor of a local newspaper and a man whose sympathies lay with the striking miners. He paraded the immigrants along the city streets and placed them in the hands of union agitators, who imprisoned them in Puddler's Hall for two days. On Sunday, March 23, John Raney, the mayor of Youngstown, accompanied by a squadron of police and mine owners, freed the Italians and convinced them to go back to Coalburg.

Early Sunday morning, a train bearing a large number of passengers pulled out of Youngstown and headed for Coalburg. Among them were the leaders of the Mahoning Coal Company: Richard Brown, his brother Thomas, Clark Powers and A.B. Cornell.[198] These men had masterminded the plan to hire the Italians, and they were determined to protect their new recruits. Aware of the movements of the coal operators, the striking miners planned to attack the encampment set up for the immigrants in Coalburg. Fassett was also on the train, and as it approached its destination, he was warned against trespassing on company property. But Fassett wasn't easily intimidated. When the train reached the station, he strode fearlessly into the coal camp.[199] Richard Brown immediately accused the newspaperman of trespassing and ordered him to leave. Upon Fassett's hesitation, the Brown brothers choked him, with Thomas raising a fist and shouting, "Shall I kill you?"[200] The men marched their captive a few yards and pushed him off their property. Fassett was promptly arrested for disturbing the peace, and Richard Brown was later charged with assault and battery. A shaky peace was imposed, and the strikers gave way to their replacements. The Italians, under police protection, were put to work digging coal. The experimental introduction of foreign workers was, for the moment, a success. The *Mahoning Vindicator* rejoiced "this action of the Mahoning Coal Company has done more to revive the spirit of business in this valley than anything that has occurred since the commencement of the strike three months ago."[201] The Coalburg operators could claim a first victory in the conflict, but the war was hardly finished.

DESPERATION AND VIOLENCE IN TRUMBULL COUNTY

During the long winter, the Church Hill strikers suffered even more than those in Coalburg. On March 12, 1873, the families of several dozen striking miners were thrown out of their homes in a raging blizzard. An agreement, signed previously by the miners as a condition of occupancy, allowed the Church Hill Coal Company to repossess their buildings. Sheriff J.W. Brooks, accompanied by two deputies, gravely executed the

> # Holmes County Republican,
> ## Thursday, April 24, 1873.
> ## A special says the coal strikers last Saturday night burned two houses at Coalburg, Ohio, the property of the Mahoning Coal Company.

Arson by striking miners. *From the* Holmes County Republican, *April 24, 1873, Chronicling America, the Library of Congress.*

court-ordered ejections. Andrew Roy observed, "The strikers may be in the wrong in refusing to accept the twenty cents reduction proposed by the operators, but it is a hard way to convince them of the fact by turning their poor helpless wives and little ones out of doors."[202] The merciless evictions enraged the strikers, who swiftly retaliated against the company.

> *A large house belonging to the Church Hill Coal Company, at Church Hill, was burned to the ground Monday night. It had been occupied by two or three families, miners, who are on a strike, and they were recently ejected by the company. The utter failure of the strikers to prevent the imported men from working, and their gloomy prospects generally, have caused a division among themselves....The burning of the house is thought to have been done by the adverse party.*[203]

Driven by desperation and anger, the frustrated strikers soon launched more attacks against the owners and the replacements at other mining camps throughout Trumbull County. On April 18, barely two weeks after the Church Hill fire, a pair of buildings at the Long Bank in Coalburg was burned to the ground.[204] The structures belonged to the Mahoning Coal Company; arson by striking miners was suspected.

John Cannif operated a boardinghouse in Vienna, a small mining camp north of Church Hill. He was also a miner who had walked off the job in January. When he returned to the mines in April, heedless of the warnings from his comrades, a party of strikers attacked his house, breaking down the door and shattering windows.[205]

On Saturday, May 10, a shot was fired into the home of Ephraim Goudge, a Liberty Township miner who had returned to work. The bullet narrowly missed his wife. Then, on Monday, May 12, strikers attempted to set fire to a house in Church Hill. Alert policemen thwarted the attempt. That night, shots were fired into three Church Hill homes occupied by strikebreakers. Also on Monday, John Evans, a non-striking miner, was stoned in Vienna in Trumbull County.[206] On May 13, strikers in Church Hill succeeded in burning another house, and at dusk, a nightlong barrage of gunfire began with the goal of intimidating those not supporting the miners' labor action.

8

DEFEAT

ADDITIONAL IMMIGRANT ARRIVALS

As winter gave way to spring, the miners' walkout continued in the Mahoning Valley. Yet its impact on the coal and iron industries was gradually diminishing as more replacements were hired from New York and Virginia. Demoralized strikers began returning to work. Not only Italian but also Swedish and German immigrants were now arriving at the mines. Rumors abounded that mine owners were sending a thousand more men to the Mahoning Valley coalfields.[207]

Encouraged by the successful introduction of immigrants to Coalburg, the Church Hill Coal Company joined the battle by recruiting more than a hundred Italians and a few Germans at Castle Garden and shipped them directly to its mine in Liberty Township. On Monday, May 12, 1873, the detachment arrived by train, and it went to work the next morning.[208]

After the arrival of the new recruits, the police and newspaper reporters closely monitored the situation in Church Hill. As the foreigners went for their picks and shovels, threats against them filled the air, but the entrance to the mine was guarded by detectives and forbidden to all outsiders. The owners were pleased by the resumption of business and requested an additional 350 men from New York. Meanwhile, reports from Hubbard Township indicated that the Coalburg Italians were mastering their new trade. They appeared satisfied with the work and remuneration provided by the coal operators.[209]

To the embittered strikers of Church Hill, the coming of the immigrants was the death knell of their cause. Unable to settle their dispute with the coal company and blindsided by the arrival of so many replacement workers, the miners turned their anger on the foreigners. Indeed, the presence of aliens in the coalfields ignited xenophobia among the workmen, who saw the newcomers overturning the established relation between miners and their workplace. It's not difficult to see how the mining community at Church Hill would seize on ethnic and other differences between the miners and the foreigners, who were Catholic and non-English speaking. It wasn't long before these resentments turned violent.

Hours after one of the Church Hill coal pits reopened, a striking miner drew a revolver on a replacement worker. The former was immediately arrested, brought before a justice of the peace and charged with assault with intent to kill. Prompted by growing tensions, additional deputies were mobilized to keep the peace. Seventy policemen from Youngstown and fifty from Cleveland descended on the mining camp.[210]

The owners' determination and skill in the use of replacement workers had succeeded. The arrival of the second group of Italians marked the end of the importations, since no more strikebreakers were needed. The tactic of importing Italians and other immigrants had crushed the colliers' resolve; their battle was lost. Just one day after the replacements began working in Church Hill, the operators permitted large numbers of defeated strikers to enter the coal banks in Coalburg and Brookfield. Within a week, coal miners across the Mahoning Valley were going back to work. When a sufficient number of men returned to work in Church Hill, the mine owners let go of the Italians. The May 21, 1873 *Cleveland Daily Plain Dealer* reported, "The last importation of emigrants which came last week have left the mines, having been provided by the operators with work on the new railroads and elsewhere." Cars filled with coal were soon rumbling along the rail lines. The strategy of the owners broke the back of the strike. Nine days after the arrival of the second group of Italians, the miners' struggle was over.

The strike in the Tuscarawas Valley ended on April 30, 1873, with both sides giving ground. Before they walked off the job, the men had been earning $1 a ton. When they asked for $1.10, the operators countered with a pay cut to 90¢.[211] The parties agreed on a wage of 95¢, and the standoff was ended.[212]

The miners in the Mahoning Valley fared worse than their counterparts in the Tuscarawas collieries. After four months of sacrifice, the strikers had gained nothing. With the walkout disintegrating around them, a final attempt was made to clinch a deal with the operators. The men offered to accept the owners' pay cut with a ten-cent raise in thirty days. They also requested that the leaders of the strike be allowed to resume their old jobs in the banks. The operators flatly refused to accept either condition. Workers would be paid ninety cents a ton, the reduction set by the operators before the strike began.[213] The few men who returned to work before the arrival of the stand-ins were permitted to keep their jobs. More than two-thirds of the striking miners held out until the end. For them, the mines were closed forever.[214]

An unintended outcome of the strike was the loss of Youngstown's dominance over the Cleveland market. The sudden shortage of coal from the Mahoning Valley forced consumers to seek other sources of fuel. It was thought that block coal was necessary to make No. 1 iron, but manufacturers discovered that inferior grades from Pittsburgh produced an acceptable substitute.[215] In the middle of the walkout, the editor of the *Cleveland Daily Leader* warned the strikers of the futility of their action. "The theory of the miners that they are bringing Cleveland to the rack is a mistake." Their stoppage, according to the *Leader*, was forcing customers in Cleveland to buy coal from other producers, including those in the Hocking Valley. "Once, this strike would have left Cleveland helpless, but that day is past."[216] Two years later, when a subsequent strike halted coal production in the Mahoning Valley, the paper reminded the Mahoning workers that Cleveland had already established contacts with other coal suppliers. Youngstown had lost its reputation as a reliable source of coal. "Time was when a miners' strike in the Mahoning Valley was a serious matter to this city, but it is no longer. The fatuity of the miners killed the goose which laid their golden egg."[217]

The strike was over, but the union men demonstrated continued hostility, especially toward the Italians. There was a feeling in the coal community that the Italians were the most to blame for the collapse of the strike, this despite the numbers of blacks, Germans and Swedes among the replacements. As a consequence, the Italians suffered daily assaults and abuse from former strikers. The worst incident occurred in the summer of 1873, when tensions boiled over and a confrontation turned deadly at a miners' bivouac in Church Hill.

A BRUTAL LYNCHING

For some time, bad blood had existed between the strikers and the Italians in Church Hill. At the conclusion of the failed strike, Scottish and Welsh miners were among those denied readmission to their old jobs. Hatred of the Italians reached a fever pitch at the Blocks, a miners' camp run by the Church Hill Coal Company. One building on the premises housed a German named Alexander Buschk and eight Italians, all of whom were immigrants and strikebreakers. For weeks, the houses sheltering the foreigners had been stoned and posted notices had warned them to leave the country. On July 27, 1873, Giovanni Chiesa (John Church) went to the well to draw water. He was confronted by a Scottish miner, William Trotter, who ordered the Italian to leave. In the ensuing struggle, Trotter was stabbed in the neck. Chiesa ran back to his lodging, after which a crowd of two hundred Scottish and Welsh miners gathered, armed with knives and clubs. Buschk heard a striker shout, "if we can't stone them out, we can burn them out," at which time the house was set afire. Alarmed that the violence was careening out of control, Buschk cautioned the crowd against taking the law into its own hands. "I told the miners if the Italians had done anything wrong to get the constable; the miners replied that they would be constables themselves."[218]

At this very point, what had begun as a heated altercation crossed the line and took on the aspect of lynch law in which the rioters would move beyond becoming "the constables" to assuming the role of jury and punishers. As planned by the crowd, the flames filled the building and forced its occupants into the open, where the assailants were waiting. While the arson initially put all the boarders in jeopardy, Buschk was allowed to get out of the house unharmed after he promised not to leave or call the police. The fleeing Italians, on the other hand, were viciously attacked and suffered gashes, broken arms and fractured skulls. Salvatore Gerardo, one of Chiesa's Italian coworkers, was so savagely mauled by the lynch mob

| NAME IN FULL. | DATE OF DEATH. | | | AGE Years. | PLACE OF BIRTH. | OCCUPATION. | Disease, Direct or Indirect Cause of Death. |
	Year.	Month.	Day.				
Church Jno.	1873			70	Italy	Miner	Murdered.

Death record of John Church (Giovanni Chiesa). *Trumbull County Courthouse.*

that he lost a leg. After languishing ten months in the Liberty infirmary, he hanged himself in despair. Several victims fled to the Seceders Cemetery, where they regrouped. One thoroughly battered Italian arrived there with two broken arms.

Chiesa, as the main recipient of the throng's outlaw justice, received the worst of it. One miner clubbed him with a gun, while others beat him to the ground and struck him with bricks. A man was heard to say that Chiesa "should have been strung up."[219] When he asked for a drink of water, his assailants threw him into a muddy hole. The strikers continued beating him and then left him on the ground; within hours, he was dead.[220] According to one witness, "some little boys were switching the deceased."[221]

The details of the Chiesa case—especially that the Church Hill mob of defeated miners saw themselves as "constables" exacting summary justice on the Italians—point to the victim's brutal murder as the first fully documented lynching committed on U.S. soil against an Italian.[222]

Arrest warrants were issued, and fifteen of the rioters were apprehended, including Trotter. The suspects showed little remorse and even contempt at their hearing.[223] William and Matthew Morrison, brothers, were charged with first-degree murder. Matthew was later sentenced to five years imprisonment in the Ohio State Penitentiary.[224]

William Parton, the most notorious of the Church Hill rioters, fled into the woods after the attack on Chiesa. He eluded capture for almost eight months. Following a lead to a Pittsburgh mine, Sheriff Brooks finally caught up with the fugitive. Parton and his friends attacked Brooks, and instead of returning to Warren with the outlaw, the sheriff came back with a broken rib.[225]

ITALIANS, A RACIAL TRUMP CARD

As a group, many miners in the post–Civil War era shared the same ethnic roots and work orientation. They mostly came from the British Isles, with a great many from southern Wales, a region with a long history of coal mining and miner culture—and recently, trade union organizing. Two of the three churches in Coalburg were founded by the Welsh.[226] The *Youngstown Vindicator* reported on May 4, 1956, that in 1881, sixty Welsh immigrants arrived in Church Hill to join friends and relatives. In another comment, Andrew Roy asserted,

The Mahoning Valley miners were nearly all natives of Wales, passionately attached to combination as the only legitimate weapon the toiling masses possessed for wringing from their employers a fair and equitable share of the products of their toil. For a number of years after their settlement in the mining districts of the Mahoning Valley, the Welsh language was the only tongue heard at the miners' meetings.[227]

The shared characteristics of local miners, along with their senses of independence and agency, came to the fore in an explosive way during the 1873 strike in Trumbull County. Roy continued, "These miners were terrible fighters. It was a dangerous experiment on the part of their employers to attempt a reduction of wages without good and sufficient reasons."[228] The local business community expressed its opposition to the stalemate through the *Youngstown Vindicator* and the *Warren Western Reserve Chronicle*; the national press echoed the same concern. The pick-and-shovel workmen had their own organ, the *Miner and Manufacturer*,[229] which galvanized working-class readership in support of the walkout. The fate of the strike had clearly rested on maintaining backing from the community. Either out of fear or from a sense of solidarity based on national origin, many whites in the area initially would not have gone against the strike.

In each of the walkouts following the Civil War, Ohio miners presented a unified front to the operators. When a stoppage was declared for New Year's Day 1873, the hardened veterans once again closed ranks and steeled themselves for the struggle. The unexpected enlistment of strikebreakers threatened the success of their offensive. Eli Perkins, a reporter for the *Cincinnati Commercial*, was in Wadsworth, Ohio, covering the situation. He interviewed disgruntled workmen whose resentment was now directed at the strikebreakers. Observing the grim individuals, Perkins said, "If any good fellow should start to work without authority of the Union, if he should be caught in an ignoble attempt to be industrious, he would be waylaid and murdered."[230]

The second arrival of Italians to the Mahoning Valley, at the Church Hill mines in May 1873, brought the strikers to their knees. The introduction of the "dusky" stand-ins blindsided the miners, who were caught off guard by such a swift, massive importation of foreign replacements. These newcomers, with no local loyalties, were propelled to the coal camps by hunger and destitution experienced in a strange land. The Italians had not been miners in their home country and were even found to mine coal at a loss.[231] The value to the coal barons of the sons of Italy was the large number of idle immigrants in New York. More were arriving every day.

The speed and effectiveness with which the Italians empowered coal operators overwhelmed the strikers, who were pushed to the edge of starvation and even to the loss of their homes. The spring of 1873 saw the once-solid ranks of Welsh and Scottish colliers reenter the Church Hill coal banks as defeated men. The Italians were the key to the humiliation. The owners had played a trump card no one had seen coming.

From the beginning of the importations, not only miners but many residents in the Youngstown area had looked disapprovingly on replacement workers from Italy. In an era when aliens were viewed through a racial prism, the use of so many desperate Italian immigrants in northeast Ohio created controversy.

> *These Italians are not the style of citizens this country hankers to fill up with; but we've got these few in our midst, and what are we going to do with them? They are incapable of learning anything but organ and harp grinding; but there ain't organs and harps enough out of use to go around.*[232]

The coal operators introduced Italians to an area of the country that had never known them, apart from the racist and anti-Catholic images that circulated in the popular press. Illustrations in the penny publications of the day, where Italians often appeared as street vermin,[233] displayed a shocking otherness. Visuals made the point that they didn't act white and therefore were not part of the white community, regardless of their entry into the country as "free white persons." Matthew Frye Jacobson's informed study of immigration and race points out the dynamics of branding by association, another factor that came into play:

> *In New Orleans Italian immigrants were stigmatized in the post–Civil War period because they accepted economic niches…marked as "black" by local custom, and because they lived and worked comfortably among blacks.*[234]

This racial typecasting of Italian immigrants as less than white must have hit a resounding note the moment the immigrants arrived as part of the same recruiting drive as the African American strikebreakers sent to New Lisbon.[235] The association of Italians with blacks in a strike-defeating, invading labor force most likely pushed the animosity felt by strikers to a deeper, more dangerous level. For many decades following, the word "scab" was spoken in the same sentence with "Italian" and "Negro."

ALONZO FASSETT, THE COAL MINERS' FIREBRAND

In the 1870s, Alonzo D. Fassett cut a figure as an ambitious and energetic political player. He was elected to the Ohio State Senate in 1879, and within four years, Governor Joseph B. Foraker appointed him state commissioner of labor. But prior to his political life, he was a pioneering newspaper editor in Hubbard, Ohio, where he devoted himself to the cause of the Trumbull County coal miners. In this, he played an outsized role in the 1873 strike.

Alonzo Fassett. *From* A History of the Coal Miners, *University of Michigan.*

Years earlier, in 1868, twenty-two-year-old Alonzo found himself wandering through Hubbard Village. He had arrived penniless and without any prospects. Picking up a local newspaper, he saw how the press demonized coal miners who were demanding higher wages. He determined that they needed a spokesman, so he started his own weekly publication by soliciting money from advertisers. He called it the *Sentinel*, and it debuted as the first newspaper in Hubbard. On its pages, he routinely supported the miners and attacked the coal operators, who had been steadily consolidating their power. In fact, he later would become an advocate of the Miners' National Association. The *Sentinel* eventually achieved a circulation of almost three thousand subscribers. In February 1869, Fassett bought his own printing press and renamed his publication the *Miners' Journal*. At the 1870 Miners' and Laborers' Benevolent Union convention, held in Youngstown, the assembled body designated Fassett's newspaper the "miners' official organ."[236] This status was reaffirmed the following year.[237]

In November 1872, Fassett purchased the *Youngstown Courier*, relocated his business there and renamed his journal the *Miner and Manufacturer*. Six months later, he changed the name of his newspaper again, this time to the *Daily Miner and Manufacturer*. It was the first daily newspaper printed in the Mahoning Valley.[238]

Fassett's partisan editorials made him popular among his working-class readers. At the same time, his tirades earned the editor the animosity of other regional newspapermen. Among them were James H. Odell and Oliver P. Wharton, the editors of the competing *Mahoning Vindicator* newspaper. On

October 17, 1873, Wharton called Fassett's *Daily Miner and Manufacturer* "the Daily Misprint and Misrepresenter."

Several of Fassett's heavy-handed pieces were aimed at Richard Brown when the aforementioned owner of the Mahoning Coal Company decided to enter the political arena. On August 1, 1872, Brown accepted the Democratic Party's nomination as candidate for the Seventeenth Congressional District of Ohio.[239] In a display of sheer opportunism and false advertising, his campaign associated itself with the "tin bucket brigade," a political organization composed entirely of workingmen.[240] Fassett was quick to seize on the apparent incongruity of Brown's platform. Less than two weeks before the election, he published his opinion of candidate Brown in the *Miners' Journal*:

> *The idea of a rich coal operator and iron manufacturer—an enemy of the miners' bill—a man who would deny his workmen the right to live and labor, except in a region surrounded by the mephitic blasts of death— claiming to be a representative working man, is so monstrously absurd that even money, the God of the capitalist, cannot bring "laboring gentlemen" to a knowledge of the truth.*[241]

Odell forcefully retorted, "The Hubbard *Journal* is violently opposed to Richard Brown, and misses no opportunity to misrepresent and malign him to the coal miners."[242]

Brown lost his congressional bid in the election held on October 8, 1872. Fassett's unsympathetic articles, read by thousands of Mahoning Valley voters, certainly played a part in Brown's defeat. Five months later, the hostility between the two men erupted in a violent encounter at the works of the Mahoning Coal Company in Coalburg. Richard and his brother, Thomas, were there to ensure the Italian replacement workers would not be harassed by the rabble. When Alonzo Fassett strode into their midst, he was assaulted by the Brown brothers, who unleashed their pent-up fury upon the journalist.

In the wake of the failed strike of 1873, tensions came to the fore within the miners' organization over the role Fassett had played. When the miners' strike initially broke out in January of that year, the newspaperman acted as the self-appointed spokesman for the miners, redoubling his harangues against the coal barons. Angered by Fassett's increasingly vituperative editorials, the paper's advertisers marched into his office and threatened to withdraw their business. Fassett ordered them out of the building; in doing so, he stiffened the backs of his readers and strengthened the resolve of the miners.

On March 31, 1873, a would-be assassin allegedly drew a pistol on Fassett, firing a shot at his head. The bullet passed through his hat, leaving the intended victim uninjured. In his *Mahoning Vindicator*, Odell reported the incident and cast doubt on the published story. The newspaper owner questioned how the gunman could have missed the intended target at a range of only eight feet. On April 18, 1873, Odell also noted that Fassett and his two bodyguards, who fired twelve shots at the "villain," had somehow completely missed the man. Did he stage the gunfight to enhance his support and hurt the coal owners? Odell appeared to suggest as much when he wrote on April 11, 1873: "Fassett, who was shot at last and missed knows exactly how he was missed. It is a good thing to know that he knows something."

Continuing into the spring of 1873, the deadlock between the miners and owners showed no signs of ending. Frustrated by the stalemate, the commitment of the strikers soon began to falter, and some of Fassett's allies abandoned him and his cause. David Owens was a local leader of the Youngstown miners who supported their walkout. As such, he might have initially been one of Fassett's supporters. With the resolution of the strike at an impasse, Owens turned against the fiery newspaper owner, saying, "the sooner Fassett 'goes up the smoke-stack,' the sooner it will suit him and a majority of the miners of the Mahoning Valley."[243]

Both men supported the miners, but their motivations appeared to be divergent, given what we know about the activities of these two leaders. Owens devoted himself to the betterment of his fellow miners, as evidenced by his fight to improve mine ventilation. Their safety was an important concern for him. Fassett supported the miners but perhaps with a view to increasing the circulation of his newspaper. While Owens rose within the ranks to earn the leadership of the miners, Fassett simply appointed himself as their spokesman. His grandstanding editorials ultimately incurred the wrath of his critics.

The strike in the Mahoning Valley crippled foundries in Cleveland that relied heavily on Trumbull County coal. As the editor of the *Cleveland Daily Plain Dealer* noted, "Cleveland is more deeply interested in this warfare than any other place and the miners have made it a point in their strike to prevent if possible coal from coming to this city."[244] Even in faraway Kansas, the *Emporia News* was attuned to the city's woes when it stated on February 14, 1873, that "Cleveland is suffering from a strike of the coal miners in the Mahoning and Tuscarawas valleys." The March 2, 1874 *Cleveland Leader* scorned the striking miners as fools "who follow the lead of such pestilent meddlers as…Fassett," a "paid mischief-maker." Three months after the strike failed, the editor of the *Leader* looked back bitterly at the role Fassett had played in the event. On September 4, 1873, it published a scathing condemnation of Fassett and his newspaper, attacking the *Daily Miner and Manufacturer* for promoting a strike that had seriously—perhaps permanently—damaged markets for local coal. The paper railed at Fassett for circulating "the thinnest, weakest and most puerile daily newspaper ever published in America." According to the *Leader*, Fassett "was mainly responsible for precipitating and prolonging the strike of the coal miners in the Mahoning Valley," the result of which paralyzed the iron industry of Youngstown. The exhortation of the miners to violence, the reduction of their families to poverty and their final, humiliating defeat—all of these things were blamed on Fassett.[245] It appears that Alonzo Fassett, attempting to build a miners' union through editorializing, provided leadership for the miners' walkout. The result was a bitter failure.

Even after the collapse of the strike, the *Daily Miner and Manufacturer* continued to serve as a union mouthpiece.[246] However, the inauguration of the *Youngstown Weekly Tribune* in September 1874 depleted Fassett's readership, and within two months, his newspaper ceased to exist. Weeks after its demise, the steadfast newsman was hired as city editor of the left-leaning *Tribune*, which was soon rechristened the *Register and Tribune*. His columns drew the ire of William Brown, the proprietor of the new *Mahoning Valley Vindicator*. Brown frequently attacked Fassett as shoddy and dishonest. In the September 17, 1875 edition of the *Vindicator*, Brown announced that the attempted assassination of Fassett two years earlier was a farce. An unnamed source claimed that, on the evening of March 31, 1873, Fassett placed his hat on a post and ordered one of his employees to shoot a hole in it. According to Brown, Fassett used the incident in an attempt to resuscitate his faltering campaign. Afterward, Brown would often use the slogan "shoot that hat" whenever he wished to emphasize one of Fassett's indiscretions.[247]

MINERS' EFFORT TO FORGE A NATIONAL UNION

Stunned by the abject failure of their campaign and eager to see comprehensive mining regulation pass various state legislatures, the defeated miners regrouped. The operators had dealt with the disorganized workers piecemeal. Seeing this, the men realized they needed to speak with a unified voice. Their goal was the formation of an organization of American

Miners' National Association at the Iron Boilers Hall, October 13, 1873. *From the* United Mine Workers Journal, *February 10, 1916, New York Public Library.*

miners joined in a centralized, nationwide union. With this aim, workers across the Midwest gathered at the Iron Boilers Hall in Youngstown, Ohio, on October 13, 1873. Under the leadership of John Siney, the Miners' National Association (MNA) was born before the meeting adjourned. The organization would fight on behalf of miners to secure benefits and provide safe working conditions. The newly minted alliance adopted the motto "In Union There Is Strength."[248]

Within two years, membership in the MNA grew to almost thirty-five thousand miners from the central coal-producing states.[249] The organization had the potential to become a powerful force for the rights of the miners, but its influence quickly disintegrated. An economic downturn in the closing months of the year, soon to be known as the Panic of 1873, lessened the demand for coal. This put the coal miners at a disadvantage for several years, as the economy fell into a lengthy depression. In the following year, the operators in the Tuscarawas Valley proposed a pay cut that was opposed by the miners. During the negotiations, the miners lost confidence in the MNA when it failed to maintain their wages. The final blow came in 1875, when Siney and his associates were ensnared in legal trouble. As the membership became demoralized, the MNA quickly faded to insignificance.

"A TERROR TO STRIKERS"

In the spring of 1872, a labor dispute was handled in a way that set a precedent for other work-related conflicts, including the 1873 coal miners' strike in northeast Ohio and northwest Pennsylvania.

Emile Grisar was a wool dealer in San Francisco from the 1850s until his death in 1882. He was regarded as "the highest authority" in California's wool industry,[250] yet by 1872, his operation was unable to supply most of his forty-five hands with a full day's work. On the morning of May 16, 1872, his underpaid employees demanded a wage increase and struck when he refused to yield.[251] He immediately replaced them with a team of immigrants. At midday, the strikers congregated at the factory and threatened the rookies with violence. When a squad of policemen appeared, the disgruntled men skulked into a nearby saloon, where they "contented themselves in idleness by drinking and watching the labors of their successors."[252] The stand-ins Grisar hired were Italians, and in employing them, the wool dealer likely became the first employer in U.S. history to enlist Italians as strikebreakers.

Two months later, the example set by Grisar was repeated in New York when workers at the Long Island Railroad struck for higher wages. After firing the malcontents, the yardmaster engaged a group of Italians to take their place. The frustrated strikers attacked their replacements, who were savagely beaten until the police intervened.[253]

On March 18, 1873, two thousand Irish laborers marched through New York City protesting their replacement by Italians hired at lower wages. Victims of a changing economy, the Irishmen were held at bay by a phalanx of policemen.[254] Meanwhile, a few blocks away, the Castle Garden bureau was the setting for a contract between a hundred Italian immigrants and the Mahoning Coal Company.

The Mahoning Coal Company's recruitment of Italian strikebreakers was the third known instance of its kind, yet a key aspect set it apart from the previous two: it was the first time Italian immigrants were contracted, transported and housed at a worksite that was significantly far from the initial point of contact. The transfer of the immigrants from the Castle Garden station to the mines of Trumbull County, a distance of four hundred miles, was an expensive undertaking that required considerable planning.

During the miners' strike of 1873, the events in the Mahoning Valley were telegraphed daily to newspapers across the United States. Employers and managers across the country watched as the mine owners outmaneuvered the striking workers. A new dynamic had tipped the old balance in favor of management, and the example was not lost on the industrial sector.

Three weeks after the first Italians left Castle Garden for the Ohio coalfields, a second group was hired to replace strikers in the New York City gasworks. Whether this action was inspired by the success of the Mahoning Coal Company or was an independent event is unclear. Either way, it demonstrated a growing awareness of the untapped labor pool on Ward's Island, where recent arrivals from Italy were housed at public expense.

On March 25, 1873, a headline in the *New York Herald* asked two questions: "Will the gas men strike? Will the city be wrapped in darkness?" Anxious residents and businessmen were nervous about the prospect. The city's gas workers, over a thousand in number, were fuming over a recent wage cut and were threatening to strike. Every business, whether a hotel, a bank or a saloon, relied on the flickering glow of gas lamps for light. Cornelius Everitt, the president of the New York Gas Company, was aware of the panic a gas shortage would cause. He ordered the construction of bunks and a kitchen on his property. These would house and feed replacement workers in the event of a walkout. He secretly recruited a company of men who would come at his command. Everitt told a reporter that the public shouldn't worry about a walkout. He bragged, "we can get plenty of new men, more than we want."[255]

On April 5, 1873, an ultimatum from the gas men was delivered to Everitt, who immediately sacked all of them. The angry workers streamed into the streets and threatened to cut the gas mains.[256] A squad of policemen was stationed around the plant to keep an eye on the mob. Meanwhile, Everitt called up the "new men" he contracted several days earlier. They were a group of sixty Italian, Swiss and German immigrants, and they were sent to the gasworks at once.

Also fearing a strike, the Manhattan Gas Company followed Everitt's example by hiring its own cadre of Italians from Ward's Island.[257] The acquisition of the men was handled by societies created to benefit the immigrants. The company's request for strikebreakers resulted in "offers from three different associations of this kind."[258] The Italians were already in place when the company dismissed the workmen on Saturday morning. At two o'clock in the afternoon, gas men armed with pistols and clubs attacked the Italians.[259] The police were quickly summoned to restore order.

The immigrants were eager to work but had no experience in the manufacture of gas. In addition, they were unable to understand the orders of the foremen. As a result, the quantity of gas produced on Sunday and

Monday was far below normal. On the streets, the strikers grinned as gas lamps flickered and went out. Yet despite the obstacles, the determined immigrants persevered. Their efficiency slowly improved, and on Tuesday, the supply of gas began to increase.[260] By the end of the week, it was clear the walkout had failed.

The strike, the ultimate weapon of the laborer, had been neutralized. Management had discovered a more powerful force by which it could ruthlessly eliminate rebellious workers. The starving immigrant, so recently a financial burden, was now a valuable resource. As one newspaper reported, "The wretched Italians…had supplanted the regular and skilled gasmen and had furnished a temporary expedient to 'beat' strikes."[261] Imbued with intelligence and tenacity, the "pauper population on Ward's Island" had proven its worth. "Could any other force have triumphed over this strike? It is safe to say no."[262]

At the April 11 meeting of the Workingmen's Trade Unions of the State of New York, a delegation of New York City gas men proposed a resolution that was unanimously adopted by the membership. The resolution was titled "No Pauper Labor Wanted In New York," and it decreed "the action of the Commissioners of Emigration in importing paupers to our shores to prey on honest labor is a crime."[263]

A newspaper reporter who covered the standoff noted the change in the equilibrium between the managers and the workers:

> There is one phase of the movement which is worthy of the attention of those studying industrial questions—that the Italians have again been taken from the care of the State, and over one hundred of them placed in an employment where they will be able to earn their own bread and raiment. Ward's Island thus proves a terror to "strikers."[264]

In the years that followed, Italian immigrants from Castle Garden were sent across the country wherever there was a need for cheap labor. They were often exploited by unscrupulous owners who used them to force striking workers to accept their demands. In April 1874, the New York Italian Labor Company was established to protect Italian immigrants from such unfair labor practices. Despite its name, the company had no connection to Italy, nor were its founders Italians. The company achieved its reputed goal by holding power of attorney over its workers and negotiating labor contracts for them. Company superintendent Frederick Guscetti said, "As peaceable and industrious men, we claim the right to put such price upon our labor as may seem to us best."[265] Those prices almost always undercut the higher wages paid to American workers, setting the stage for inevitable strife.

In September 1874, coal miners struck the Armstrong Works at Buena Vista in Allegheny County, Pennsylvania. The proprietors immediately contacted the New York Italian Labor Company, which sent nearly two hundred immigrant workers.[266] Newspaper editor Frank Cowan declared, "In resolving to employ Italian laborers in their mines, the coal operators of Pittsburgh are striking the boldest blow against the well organized Miners' Union of this city it has ever received."[267]

The responses from the miners' organizations to this action were predictable. The indignant editor of the *National Labor Tribune*, the official voice of the colliers, vehemently opposed the importation of the Italians.[268] The publisher declared, "Not a bushel of coal should be dug until every last greasy wretch is sent out of the county. The operators who have imported them should be black-listed, and not a bushel of coal allowed to be taken from their banks for six months after the Italians are expelled."[269]

Also predictable was the ensuing violence directed at the immigrants. Two months of smoldering tensions erupted into open warfare on the night of November 28, 1874, when two hundred heavily armed men laid siege to the Italian encampment. All night and most of the next day, bullets flew across the Youghiogheny River, which became the frontier of battle. When the shooting finally stopped, three Italians were dead.[270]

Early in 1875, dissatisfaction over wages was growing once again in the coal camps of northeast Ohio. In March, John Siney, president of the Miners National Association, encouraged a walkout in the Tuscarawas Valley.[271] On April 2, five hundred miners from the Mahoning and Shenango Valleys met in Youngstown to consider joining the Tuscarawas stoppage. Many of the men were angry with Siney "for starting this strike in the interest of the Tuscarawas Valley."[272] Nevertheless, Youngstown area colliers soon joined the stoppage.

Many of the coal banks in Pennsylvania were also shut down. In the middle of May 1875, operators considered bringing German substitutes to the Franklin works in Tyrone, and it was rumored that Italians would be brought to a mine in Clearfield.[273] Anticipating trouble, the Italian consul in Philadelphia telegraphed the Clearfield sheriff with a request for protection of the immigrants.[274] Xingo Parks, an organizer for the Miners' National Association, was in the coalfields to rally the strikers. Commenting on the speculation that Italian strikebreakers would be introduced to the district's mines, he warned,

The fight is no longer for ten cents advance, it is for the perpetuity of the union. If the Italians come up from Tyrone tomorrow I cannot be responsible for the consequences. We do not know their language nor they ours, and cannot reason with them. Our men, therefore, will be likely to adopt other means.[275]

On May 18, Parks hurriedly left the area, pursued by the authorities with warrants for his arrest.[276] He was apprehended at Osceola, Pennsylvania, and brought to Clearfield, where he was tried and convicted of conspiracy and unlawful assemblage.[277]

Siney was also indicted and tried for conspiracy in the Clearfield incident. He knew the owners had no expectations the immigrants would efficiently mine coal. It's an established fact that there are no deposits of carboniferous minerals, save lignite and peat, on the Italian peninsula.[278] Instead, the labor leader believed the Italians were mercenaries in a counter-offensive. "The importation of Italians and others with no mining experience, and who could not mine coal without a loss, was part of a scheme of the operators to exhaust the funds of the strikers in paying the fares of the new comers back again."[279] Siney's declaration echoed a widely held belief made during the previous year's importation of Italians at Buena Vista:

In the face of their desire to adjust wages to the condition of the market, foreigners who never saw a coal mine are imported, and for what? To dig coal? No. It is not pretended they can dig. But they propose to learn them. These operators know all the coal they dig for the next six months will cost them more than our miners will work for. This is only an attempt to so utterly demoralize our union men that they will surrender the organization at once and forever.[280]

In early June, the miners conceded defeat, thus ending what was known as the Long Strike.[281] As in the walkout of 1873, the Italians were hated not only for being strikebreakers but also for their use as strategic weapons in the operators' war against coalfield trade unions. Welshmen of the time faced no greater danger than a contingent of Italians sent by coal operators to starve them out and bust their union.

Immigrants were rapidly becoming the laborers of choice for thrifty employers. In New York City, groups of foreigners were often managed by a labor contractor who leased them to work at railroads, shipyards or

Starving miners appeal to James Blaine as Italians march into the Hocking Valley. *From Puck, October 15, 1884, Library of Congress, Prints and Photographs Division.*

public works. Because so few Italians spoke English, they had to be hired in "gangs" that included one interpreter. Trouble always followed when these organized contingents of immigrants replaced striking workers. In November 1874, ten thousand longshoremen triggered a work stoppage at the New York docks.[282] When companies of Italians arrived to replace them, strikers bullied and beat the hated replacements. The newcomers once more suffered the consequences of accepting work in a hostile environment.

By 1884, mine management had turned to employing Italian strikebreakers on a routine basis. Yet the shock value of hordes of immigrants marching into idle mines had lost none of its sensationalism or dread. At this time, the Hocking Valley was Ohio's chief coal-producing region. In April of that year, Hocking coal operators announced that a reduction in wages was necessary to remain competitive with suppliers from Pennsylvania and Indiana. Their employees threatened a walkout. The cut was implemented on June 20; three days later, the men abandoned the shafts.[283] The operators lost no time recruiting squads of Italians to step into the breach. On July 13, 250 Italians were brought to the coal camp, escorted by 100 special police and 30 Pinkerton detectives. A baggage car loaded with guns and ammunition accompanied the men.[284] At first, the miners laughed to see inexperienced foreigners handling picks and shovels. But their smiles faded as the weeks dragged on and the immigrants dug for coal. An attack was planned, and on Saturday evening, August 30, the strikers and guards exchanged gunfire. Over a thousand rounds were fired between the opponents. When the shooting stopped, several combatants were wounded, and one guard lay dead.[285] Six months of simmering acrimony followed the riot. After a nine-month struggle, the strikers acknowledged failure, and on March 18, 1885, they accepted the operators' terms.[286] The immigrants had become the bogeymen of the unions, for the foreigners' presence all too often meant calamity for the striking workforce.

The practice of using pauper labor from outside the British Isles to cow or replace semi- and unskilled American workers became a frequently used option. Often, employers simply bypassed the local workforce by hiring immigrants. Years after the 1873 strike, Youngstown was again put on edge by the threat of foreign labor. The *Youngstown Evening Vindicator* of April 30, 1890, gave credence to a rumor that "two car loads of Italians arrived here last night from the East" to build tracks for the New York, Pennsylvania & Ohio Railroad Company. The editor decried the idea—"We have lots of idle men in this vicinity, who would be glad to find employment without importing this pauper labor from the East, to overflood our place."

Despite the very disadvantageous position in which early immigrant laborers found themselves, it didn't take long for some of them to organize and respond to management exploitation. The spring of 1886 saw fifty former strikebreakers in Edinburg, Pennsylvania, all Italian quarrymen, lead a walkout to secure pay on a par with that of American workers. The strike campaign visited worksites from heavily Italian Lawrence County, Pennsylvania—where the Hillsville and Carbon limestone quarries were located—to Brier Hill and Lowellville in Mahoning County.[287]

CONCLUSION

In the fall of 1872, several thousand impoverished Italians left Italy for the United States, including the wayfarers from Agnone. These were the shiploads of unfortunates who had escaped the crushing poverty of their homeland only to encounter an uncertain future in an America not yet familiar with Southern Europeans. Lacking job prospects and contacts in America, they were housed for months at public expense in New York

City. Their unexpected influx caught the attention of the media, and from November 1872 until January 1873, headlines about the migrants appeared almost daily in newspapers across the country. Coverage of the crisis culminated at the end of January in a war of words between Joseph McDonnell, a reporter for the *New York Herald*, and Francis Hurst, manager of the National Line of steamers. The newspaperman's exposé of passenger abuse on the *Erin*, a vessel operated by Hurst's scandal-plagued company, revealed the extreme suffering experienced by its Italian passengers.

But by the second week of February, the immigrants had vanished from the pages of American journals. All but forgotten, they seemed destined to be marginalized. Yet events soon put them on a national stage. Two hundred of them answered the call to work the struck mines in Coalburg and Church Hill, where the displaced exiles of this story landed not in the melting pot of a welcoming nation but in the fiery cauldron of a coal war in the Mahoning Valley. As such, they became the first group of Italians to settle there and were probably the first Italian strikebreakers to enter a U.S. coal mine.

The catastrophic failure of the 1873 coal miners' strike created tremors that rippled far beyond the Mahoning Valley.[288] Across the country, subsequent miners' walkouts collapsed when employers sidestepped their workers and hired Italian immigrants from Castle Garden and blacks from the South. Chauncey Andrews set the example of looking outside the area for replacements, and other operators took the further step of hiring foreign, pauper labor. These novel strategies furthered the coal companies' attempts to win the greater war, the end of union power in the nation's coalfields. The ultimate goal of the owners, as declared by William Powers, was "to protect our interests, to burst the Miners' Union, and see that no man in sympathy with them, or who has made threats, gets employment."[289]

Twenty years later, the business of recruiting Italian immigrants for mine work was flourishing. The practice became so lucrative that some mine owners employed agents whose only duty was the solicitation of unwitting Italian immigrants as they arrived at the barge office. Alerted by complaints, W.E. Mulholland ordered an inspection of the mining districts in western Pennsylvania early in 1892. As head of the contract labor bureau at Ellis Island, he sent a disturbing report to the U.S. House of Representatives.

An investigation has been made under the direction of the Treasury Department in the mining regions to find out how many immigrants were working there. The report of the inspectors shows that the American miner has virtually disappeared.[290]

Mulholland's account showed that Italians were crowding out American miners at an alarming rate. What began as an expedient to break a strike had devolved into the trafficking of Italian labor. Unscrupulous owners and their mercenary agents circumvented beneficial organizations intent on protecting immigrants from such exploitation. But the damage was already done. "The native American miner has almost disappeared from the coal regions of Pennsylvania."[291]

Few of the Italians who came to the Mahoning Valley in 1873 spoke English, and none were aware they were replacing striking miners until confronted by an angry mob in Coalburg. But as time passed, the situation became clear, and they perceived the injustice done to them. Two years later, when the miners struck again, William Powers asked the Italians to work in his mines. They responded that "they had 'blacklegged' once, not understanding it, but would not do so any more."[292]

Like Italians, blacks earned scorn as scabs, but they had an additional barrier to surmount. "The cynical use of African Americans, often recruited from the South, to break strikes was extremely harmful to race relations,

Coccavillan family of Youngstown, 1916. *The Mahoning Valley Historical Society.*

both immediately and extending into the 20th century."[293] Their role as scabs would haunt them and forestall their full integration into the American workforce for decades.

Before long, Italians in several areas would defend working conditions as non-strikebreakers. The precarious condition of their employment as hated strikebreakers taught them what their white counterparts had already found essential: unity on the job site. They responded to grievances with spontaneous job actions and by eventually joining trade unions. In December 1891, seventy Italians joined the strike against wage cuts demanded by the Colorado Coal and Iron Company.[294] In the South in the 1880s and 1890s, African Americans also working as miners enrolled in the United Mine Workers of Alabama.[295]

By the second half of the 1800s, iron ore from the Great Lakes region began to supplant dwindling Mahoning Valley sources of the mineral. Most coal mines in Coalburg and many in Trumbull County and the surrounding area closed in the 1880s. No matter. The blast furnaces, foundries and rolling mills that clung to the banks of the industrial waterway, the Mahoning River, had enjoyed such a productive head start that the exhaustion of local mineral resources failed to dent output. From now on, the Lake Superior area would supply ore and the Appalachians would furnish coal. Mahoning Valley industry, nurtured by the earlier coal boom, continued to expand, adding technological innovations in iron and then steel production. By World War II, from Warren, Ohio, to Sharon, Pennsylvania, the valley boasted sixty-one open hearths, twenty-five blast furnaces and three Bessemer converters.[296] As mineable coal was depleted, the area's industries focused on iron production, and the immigrant workforce adjusted to the new paradigm. Italian laborers left the coal mines and entered the steel mills.

In 1873, the Italians who answered the call from the Mahoning coal operators unknowingly stepped across a deadly line. Despite the poisoned atmosphere between English-speaking worker and immigrant resulting from the 1873 strike, the conflict was the opening act for one of the greatest waves of immigration in American history. Before the strike of 1873, there wasn't a single Italian immigrant in Mahoning County. By 1912, nearly fifteen thousand inhabited the industrial corridor stretching from the east end of Youngstown to the Brier Hill steel works.[297] Between 1880 and 1920, over four million Italians would land in the United States,[298] enriching the nation's culture and changing forever the tapestry of American life.

PART TWO: PEACE

They are generally from the country districts of Italy, who, only within two years, have found out the fact that the United States is a good country to emigrate to, and are coming every year in increasing numbers.

—Frank Cowan
"The Italians as Coal Miners"
Washington Reporter, *September 23, 1874*

9

A NEW HOME IN AMERICA

THE PANIC OF 1873 AND THE
DEPLETION OF THE MINES

The coal miners' strike of 1873 crippled the economy of the Mahoning Valley. It panicked the mine operators and devastated the coal miners. Yet, for the handful of Italian immigrants who were introduced to the mines and, later, to railroad labor, the predicament offered economic advantages: steady work at wages impossible to attain in southern Italy. Unfortunately, the good times were fleeting. The Italians and the other residents of the valley would soon face hard times.

In September 1873, a financial crisis known as the Panic of 1873 sparked an economic depression. The decline was widespread and affected all industries in the United States. Banks failed and businesses closed. The demand for iron and coal plummeted. A dark cloud settled over the Mahoning Valley. A year after the onset of the depression, a correspondent for the *Cleveland Leader* reported the effect of the downturn on the residents of Hubbard: "There are scores of men, mostly Italians, now wandering from house to house seeking work and food, who, when the winter comes on, will be in a truly deplorable condition."[299] The financial slump lingered for six years, but the mining industry of Hubbard Township never fully recovered.

Another blow to the local economy was the inevitable exhaustion of the coal reserves. The coal seams in Trumbull County were relatively easy to work. They were aggressively mined and, as a result, quickly depleted. Activity in Trumbull County peaked in 1870, when thirty-nine mines produced two million tons of coal. By 1880, only fourteen mines operated in the county, and the output of coal had fallen by almost 80 percent.[300]

Coalburg was a boomtown in the 1860s. It was a kingdom ruled by the coal monarchs of Youngstown, among whom were Chauncey Andrews, William Powers and the leaders of the Mahoning Coal Company. Hundreds of workers thronged to the place and were employed excavating hundreds of tons of coal every day. The settlement's population swelled to eight hundred in 1870, when production reached its peak. Mining began to wane in the 1870s, and as the decade drew to a close, relatively few men received a full day's work in its four remaining coal banks.[301] By 1882, the community had lost nearly two-thirds of its residents,[302] and its rapidly shrinking coal industry was insufficient to fully support the remaining workers.[303] The mines were dwindling, yet Italians still came to Trumbull County.

FROM STRIKEBREAKERS TO YOUNGSTOWN
PROMINENTI

Respected *prominenti*, or community leaders, emerged from the ranks of the early Italian community. While building contractor Louis Adovasio and others achieved renown in the next generation, by the early 1890s, three coal strike veterans—Stefano Colucci, John Gentile and Marco Antonelli—were each making news as contributors to the development of the Mahoning Valley.

Marco Antonelli

On June 30, 1873, a sixteen-year-old locksmith from Agnone boarded a steamship bound for the United States. He arrived in Youngstown on July 22, just six weeks after the end of the miners' strike.[304] Unable to speak a word of English, he went looking for a job.

> *Too young to work in the mines, he found employment at 50 cents a day at Coalburg. Later, he spent a few months in Pennsylvania, and was at Buena Vista when three Italians were killed during a strike. Returning*

*to Coalburg, he was a water boy six months, being paid 75 cents a day.
Then for the first time he became a regular miner, working on the inside.
He spent two years in and at the mines, and for two years was in the
Brown Bonnell plant.*[305]

The industrial markets in which early immigrants worked had become
increasingly contentious, and this included Liberty Township's collieries. As
the mood of the miners there became more resolute, Antonelli departed
for Italy. In October 1881, the Church Hill miners struck, demanding an
increase of fifteen cents for every ton of coal they produced. When the
owners of the Kyle, Otis and Church Hill mines hesitated, 400 employees
walked off the job.[306] It was feared the labor action would eventually spread
through the entire Mahoning Valley. Six months later, the Church Hill mines
were struck again when 350 miners walked out.[307]

On May 8, in the midst of the turmoil swirling around the strike, the
steamship *Ferdinand de Lesseps* docked in New York City with 476 passengers
aboard, of whom 457 were Italian males.[308] The manifest included at least
four passengers from Agnone with the Coalburg mining settlement as their
destination. The ship also carried Antonelli and his bride, Giovina Di
Camillo. He was returning to his job with Brown, Bonnell and Company.
The question remains whether Antonelli may have acted as a labor
contractor whose goal was, while in Italy, to recruit a workforce to keep
open the struck mines in Trumbull County.

In later years, Antonelli operated a grocery, bakery and foreign exchange
bank on East Federal Street in Youngstown. In this last capacity, he acted as
an agent for a dozen steamship companies that transported Italians to the
United States. Antonelli was a popular, civic-minded individual who gained
the respect of Youngstown's Italian community. One of the founders of Our
Lady of Mount Carmel Catholic Church in 1913, he was also one of the
first naturalized Italian citizens in the Mahoning Valley and cast his first
presidential vote for James A. Garfield in 1880.[309]

His wife, Giovina, died in 1897, and the following year, he married
Gabriella Ferrando, a widow from Coalburg. The couple eventually retired to
Antonelli's estate in Youngstown, but they retained ownership of Gabriella's
Coalburg properties, a tie that harkened back to the days when the young
immigrant from Agnone first saw Hubbard Township.

John Gentile (Salvatore Gentili)

If Antonelli achieved recognition as a self-made, successful businessman, then John Gentile—the name he used almost exclusively—attained the status of an original Mahoning Valley celebrity. There is no information about his birthplace and upbringing in Italy. Sources say that he arrived on a "strong-masted schooner,"[310] and he is found in Marco Antonelli's enumeration of the earliest Italians who worked during the coal miners' strike.[311]

Gentile's role in the four-day Monster Fair of 1891 painted him as Youngstown's master showman and outdoor food vendor. In a large ad in the August 29 *Youngstown Evening Vindicator*, he advertised a "Beer and Lunch Hall" at the festive venue scheduled for the first four days of September. The ad topped off the list of Gentile-sponsored attractions with the promised launch of an unmanned lighter-than-air-balloon of record dimensions. A reward of two dollars was offered to the lucky person who was able to report the craft's landing. To conclude the expensive newspaper piece, Gentile reminded readers to stop by his hotel to enjoy its fine stock of beverages and food.

Gentile's initiative in organizing the Società Fraterna Italiana,[312] a benefit society, underscored his leadership in the immigrant community. In an age when no health or burial insurance existed, fraternal organizations aided immigrants who lacked collateral to secure credit from banks.

In 1892, Gentile led the Italian community's participation in the elaborate parade commemorating the four hundredth anniversary of Columbus's landing in the New World. On at least one occasion, he assisted the court as an interpreter in an 1893 case of an Italian charged with murder.[313] By 1897, he was residing in Warren and opening a "fine restaurant" on North Hazel Street. The locale was no mere diner but a gourmet's delight that also stocked domestic and imported wines and cigars.[314] Gentile ended his marriage with his first wife, Jennie Mantella, in 1896, and married Mary Lewis in 1898. The businessman's marital notoriety reached scandal proportions in an era when even American-born couples seldom divorced. Gentile was an early member of Our Lady of Mount Carmel Church, Youngstown. He died in 1915 and lies buried in Calvary, Youngstown's diocesan cemetery.

Stefano Colucci

Stefano Colucci showed what an immigrant from the southern Italian countryside could accomplish. He was born in Avellino to a family of cheese makers. Seeking a better life in America, he arrived in New York on September 12, 1872. Seven months later, Colucci was still attempting to find employment there when a representative of the Mahoning Coal Company offered him a job in the firm's Trumbull County mines.[315] The newly arrived immigrant, in the company of other Italians, boarded a train bound for Ohio. His final destination was Coalburg.[316]

He was eager to do the work, but it soon became apparent that the contractor had omitted an important aspect of his employment. He and his countrymen had unknowingly been hired as strikebreakers in a protracted and violently contested work stoppage. Undaunted, he spent the next sixteen years in and around the mines. He learned the language and customs of his adopted homeland and gained the respect and trust of his fellow Italians. In 1873, his wife, Francesca Agnone, joined him. The two of them were founding members of Our Lady of Mount Carmel Church, Youngtown.

Leaving the mines, Colucci became a foreman for Dan Monahan, a Youngstown contractor. Soon the Italian opened his own contracting business. As his reputation grew, Colucci was awarded larger and more prestigious contracts. His business paved many miles of Youngstown streets and plumbed the sewers beneath them. The company built the streetcar lines that connected Youngstown, Sharon, New Castle, Wheatland and Sharpsville. Eventually becoming the wealthiest Italian in the Mahoning Valley,[317] Colucci was a prime example of what a determined immigrant could achieve in the United States. Like building contractors Louis Adovasio, Vincenzo Mango and Giuseppe Gialdini, he entered the ranks of Youngstown's influential *prominenti*. Colucci died in 1930.

THE COALBURG ITALIANS, THE MAHONING VALLEY'S FIRST ITALIAN SETTLERS

A RECORD OF THE ITALIAN SETTLEMENT

While other labor conflicts would ignite Ohio collieries, peace did come to Coalburg. By 1880, more than half of the immigrants who had so lately thronged its coalfields were gone. Some migrated to jobs in nearby towns like Sharon and Youngstown, while others may have returned to their homes across the Atlantic. A few moved to Krebs in the Indian Territory, where they joined a colony of Italian miners.

Those remaining in Coalburg continued to reside in their former mining camp, the Mahoning Coal Company's Addition to Coalburg. During the fractious Coal War, it served as the miners' barracks and the headquarters of Richard Brown and William Bonnell's mining kingdom. Some worked in the failing mines, while others turned to farming. The colony was isolated from the rest of the community, where memories were long and resentments ran deep. They were surrounded by people they had displaced in the mines—people who had given the name "Little Italy" to the immigrants' enclave.[318] Eventually, the old-time residents grudgingly accepted the Italians' presence as the acrimony of 1873 abated. The miners' strike was over, and so was a contentious era. In time, tensions faded, and the stronghold became a home. A shift in the public's attitude toward the Italians, from distaste to respect, could be glimpsed in the February 25, 1874 article "The City: Local Brevities" by the editor of the *Cleveland Leader*, who said "a number of the Italians who were the subject

"Blasting in a Coal Mine: Waiting for the Blast," 1873. *Scientific American Inc.*

of so much honest indignation last summer, are now earning an honorable living in the coal mining districts."

When the census was taken in June 1880, it indicated that ninety-two Italians were living in Hubbard Township, eighty-one of them residing on or adjacent to the addition.[319] Twenty-one of the Italian names on the census are badly misspelled and cannot be identified with any known families. However, seventy-one of the township's Italian residents are recognizable. Ten of those, including members of the Campia, Pepe and Marino families, were from the region of Campania. The Marcovecchios, Misischias, Saulinos, Menaldis and the two Carosella families were from Agnone, then in the province of Campobasso.[320] Although absent from the 1880 census, eight men from Pietrabbondante were part of the original group of settlers in 1873.[321] Including their Ohio-born children, twenty-five Agnonesi resided in Coalburg in 1880. Nothing is known of the origin of Pasquale Di Paola, a Coalburg settler. However, his close ties to Filippo and Mercede Carosella likely associate him with Agnone, bringing the total number of Agnonesi in Little Italy to twenty-six.

Many of the Coalburg residents hailed from Carovilli or its *frazione* or hamlet, Castiglione, located less than fifteen kilometers from Agnone in what was then Campobasso Province. Among the *Carovillesi*[322] was the

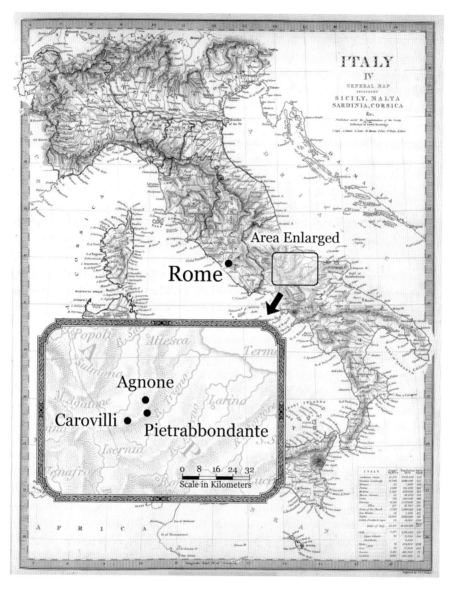

Italy, prior to Unification, modified to show Agnone, Carovilli and Pietrabbondante. *David Rumsey Map Collection, www.davidrumsey.com.*

family of Pasquale and Angela Di Giacomo. Their next-door neighbors were Gennaro Iannacone and his family, who were also from Carovilli.[323] Michele and Philomena Di Giacomo were from Castiglione, as were Donato Di Domenico and the Nuosci family. If four Di Giacomo men who were boarding with families from Carovilli and Castiglione are included, then there were thirty Carovillesi on the Coalburg census. Therefore, 69 percent of the identifiable residents of Coalburg's Little Italy hailed from the four neighboring towns of Agnone, Carovilli, Castiglione and Pietrabbondante. This unique pedigree was not the result of random emigrations. Instead, it derived from a fraudulent advertising campaign targeting Campobasso in the fall of 1872, coupled with the systematic recruitments from Castle Garden in succeeding years. The well-known phenomenon of Italian chain immigration, i.e. settling where immigrants from one's hometown could be found, also aided in building Coalburg as a destination for immigrants from Campobasso.

What follow are the family histories of Coalburg's Italians. This "Class of 1873" was sui generis.[324] No Italian community existed to welcome these immigrants or to sustain their "Italianness." There was no local Italian press, Italian merchant class or Italian-language parish in the area. The newcomers from Italy would build their own cultural infrastructure, fusing Italian traditions and midwestern ways.

Filippo and Mercede Carosella
(Phillip and Martha Carsela, 1880 census)

Pasquale Di Paola (Basqual Powell, 1880 census)

Filippo Carosella was one of the first Italians to arrive in Coalburg in the spring of 1873. Recruited to work in the mines, he continued in this occupation for at least seven years. Sometime in 1875, he was badly hurt in an accident in Coalburg's Long Bank, a mile and a half from his home in Little Italy. Caught under a fall of coal, Carosella received serious injuries to his body, arms and legs.[325] After his eventual recovery, he returned to work in the pits.

By 1880, Filippo's wife, Mercede, and children Francesco and Concetta had joined him in Coalburg. Though just fourteen years old, Francesco was already working in the mines. At that time, the couple rented rooms in their home to Italian miners, one of whom was Pasquale Di Paola. By 1889, the Carosellas had moved to Youngstown, where Filippo died sometime before June 1900. The census of that year shows Di Paola living in the same Youngstown neighborhood as the Carosellas. On February 7, 1901, he

Marriage of Philip Ferrando and Jennie Carosella, 1901. *Robert and Carole Madeline.*

married Filippo's widow, Mercede. The Youngstown City Directories listed Pasquale as a shoemaker, with a final entry for him in 1906. Whether he died in Mahoning County or repatriated to Italy is unknown. Mercede, alone again, died in Youngstown on January 6, 1929.

The bonds between Italian immigrants were strong, especially among those from the same comune. So it was with Filippo Carosella and Filippo Marcovecchio. The two Agnonesi arrived in the United States aboard the steamship *Erin* in 1873 and settled in Coalburg, where they worked together in the mines. Carosella's daughter Jennie married Marcovecchio's grandson Philip Ferrando on November 6, 1901, at St. Columba Church (later the diocesan cathedral) in Youngstown.

Alfonso and Angela Maria Saulino
(Alfons and Mary A. Soulino, 1880 census)

In 1880, Alfonso and Angela Maria Saulino were living in Coalburg. In 1884, they purchased a parcel belonging to Filippo and Merceda Marcovecchio. This was lot number two in the Mahoning Coal Company's Addition to Coalburg. The 1880 census recorded Alfonso as a shoemaker. By 1891, he operated a poolroom in Youngstown where his son, Benedict, was a bartender. From 1900 until his death in 1931, Alfonso was once again a shoemaker. According to records in *Ohio County Births, 1841–2003*, *Ohio Births and Christenings, 1821–1962* and *Ohio Deaths, 1908–1953*, three sons were born to the Saulinos in Coalburg. They had their first son, Benedict, on February 15, 1875.[326] This listing in the registry is one of the earliest known documents establishing the residence of an Italian family in Hubbard Township. Other children born to the Saulinos in Coalburg were Felix on April 6, 1878, and Frank on May 1, 1880. The couple had two children in Youngstown, Lizzie (Librett) in 1885 and Albert (who did not survive) on March 16, 1889. Angela Maria died in Youngstown on May 31, 1899.

Although Alfonso was a humble shoemaker, he was exceptionally active within his community. He established the Società Duca degli Abruzzi-Colombo, for which he received an award from the Italian government. He was also recognized as having been the first person to raise the Italian flag in Youngstown.[327]

Filippo and Merceda Marcovecchio
(Phillip and Martha Marquet, 1880 census)

Filippo Marcovecchio arrived in Coalburg on March 19, 1873. His wife, Merceda, and his daughter, Gabriella, joined him eight months later. They were among the first Italian settlers in Hubbard Township.[328] They were also the second Italian family to buy property in Little Italy. On July 26, 1878, they purchased lot number two in the Mahoning Coal Company's Addition to Coalburg. The company's president, Augustus B. Cornell, signed the deed. In the *Trumbull County Assessment of Farm Lands for 1880,* it was noted that the parcel was valued at $50.[329] On August 18, 1884, the Marcovecchios sold the land to Alfonso and Angela Maria Saulino. Four years later, on October 8, 1888, Alfonso sold it to Damiano Misischia and Joe Maddalena.

Filippo worked in a coal bank, while Merceda supplemented the family's income by operating a boardinghouse for miners, including Anthony Ferrando, a young Italian immigrant who married her daughter, Gabriella, in 1880. On May 4, 1885, Filippo Marcovecchio and Anthony Ferrando bought the entire north half of the Mahoning Coal Company's Addition to Coalburg. The sale included lots twenty through forty plus a small triangle of land on the northeast edge of the addition. According to the deed, the corners of this triangular lot were marked by two stones and "a white oak stump." The property included "a one-story frame office"[330] that once served as the headquarters of the Mahoning Coal Company, whose president, Ralph Wick, signed the deed.

Filippo Marcovecchio died in Coalburg on July 7, 1895. The cause of death was consumption, possibly a result of years spent working in the mines. Shortly after Filippo's death, Merceda married Michael Lorenzo, who died in 1902, after which she married Emidio Tenaro in 1903. Emidio's eventual fate is not known; Merceda died a widow on November 10, 1920, at the Hubbard home of her grandson, Michael Ferrando.

Anthony and Gabriella Ferrando
(Anthony Fearant and Barbra Marquet, 1880 census)

Anthony Ferrando and Gabriella Marcovecchio were married on October 23, 1880, in St. Patrick's Church in Hubbard. On their marriage application, Gabriella declared she was at least eighteen years old, but the 1880 census listed her as twelve. A newspaper article reported her as "over 40 years old" in 1898,[331] but a Youngstown historian claimed that she was "a child of six years when brought by her parents to the United States."[332] Several sources indicate her parents immigrated in 1873, so she was only twelve or thirteen years old when she married twenty-eight-year-old Anthony Ferrando in 1880. Anthony and Gabriella eventually had five children on their Coalburg farm. Philip was born in 1882, followed by Martha in 1885, Michael in 1889, Joseph in 1892 and Casimiro in 1896.

Anthony died of consumption on April 13, 1897. Gabriella was now a widow and the sole means of support for her five young children. In September 1897, five months after the death of her husband, Gabriella took in an Italian drifter named Angelo Will. He also went by Angelo Bill or Angelo Del Bello, though neither was his real name.[333] In February 1898, when Gabriella refused his proposal of marriage, Angelo attempted to kill her and the entire family. On the evening of February 24, 1898, he arrived at the Ferrando home carrying a loaded revolver. Opening fire, the gunman wounded four members of the family. Three of them survived, but Gabriella's five-year-old son, Joseph, died eight days later from a gunshot wound to his abdomen.

Michael and Philip Ferrando witnessed the tragic shooting of their younger brother, Joseph. The violent attack may have influenced the older brothers' career choices. A few years after the assault, Philip was employed at the Lake Shore & Michigan Southern Railway in Youngstown. Later, he became the third Italian American to join the city police force. On April 10, 1907, he was sworn into service.[334] He was preceded by Louis Venerose and Daniel Maggianetti on the police force. On March 26, 1919, he died from complications after an operation. In Ferrando's obituary, he was praised as a popular policeman who had gained the respect of his fellow officers.[335]

After receiving a diploma from Youngstown's Rayen High School, Michael Ferrando attended Miami University, where he received a bachelor of arts degree in 1913. He studied at the Cincinnati Law School, graduating in 1916. That same year, he established his law practice with an office in the Home Savings and Loan Building in downtown Youngstown.[336]

Damiano and Clementina Misischia
(Daniel Mishhishk, 1880 census)

Damiano Misischia immigrated in 1879. He arrived in Coalburg, where he worked as a miner while boarding with his sister, Merceda Marcovecchio. Eight years later, wife Clementina and daughter Giovanna joined him. A

Damiano, Clementina and Giovanna Misischia around 1880. *Robert and Carole Madeline.*

second daughter, Elizabeth, was born in 1892. The family stayed in Coalburg until 1900, when they moved to Hubbard. Damiano, later known as Daniel Note, operated a grocery store in the town from about 1905 until his death in 1920.

Giovanna Misischia and Giovanni Maddalena (Joe Madeline)

Giovanna Misischia married Giovanni Maddalena in January 1888. For a few years, they lived in Coalburg, where Giovanni earned a living as a coal miner. In 1893, the couple moved to Hubbard. Giovanni, known in Hubbard as "Joe," opened the Clover Leaf House, a saloon and hotel, on North Main Street in 1903. On October 28, 1908, Trumbull County voters chose to make the county dry, forcing Joe to close his establishment. Undaunted by this setback, he converted the building into a nickelodeon. Joe Madeline was a successful businessman and one of Hubbard's best-known residents. He never forgot his beginnings as an Italian immigrant in the Coalburg mines. In 1921, he and his son, Anthony, established one last enterprise. With a capital outlay of $10,000, they created the Block Coal Company, a mining and wholesale coal business.[337]

Joe Madeline's Clover Leaf House around 1905. *Phil Madeline.*

Gaetano and Maria Formichelli

Gaetano and Maria Formichelli were the first Italians to buy property in Coalburg. On June 26, 1876, they purchased a quarter of an acre of land from John Blake for sixty dollars.[338] The property was located on Great Lot 23, on the east side of Greene Street, adjacent to the eastern border of the Mahoning Coal Company's Addition to Coalburg. Gaetano and Maria's daughter, Mary, was born there on January 15, 1879. Five months after her birth, John Blake acquired the Formichelli lot. Nathaniel Mitchell, a justice of the peace and the former mayor of Hubbard, notarized the deeds for both transactions.

Sabbatius and Angelina Marino
(Sobadine and Anjulina Marian, 1880 census)

Sabbatius Marino was born in Caserta, in the region of Campania, Italy, on April 13, 1837. He married Angelina Pallerin Palmanbo in 1858. Ten years later, Angelina gave birth to a daughter, Maria, and a son, Giuseppe, in 1871. According to the 1900 census, Sabbatius immigrated to the United States in 1872. In 1880, he and his family were living in Coalburg, where he worked in the mines. Despite the closure of most of the mines, the Marinos remained in Coalburg until at least 1899. A second daughter, Rosie, was born there in 1884. By 1899, the Marino families owned almost half of the properties in the Mahoning Coal Company's Addition to Coalburg. Angelina died in Hubbard on September 13, 1913; Sabbatius died six weeks later, on October 29, 1913.

The Pepe and Campia Families:
Alessandro, Sabatino and Maria Pepe
(Aixander, Sabadean and Mary Paber, 1880 census)

Benjamin and Chancena Campia
(Benjamin and Chancena Gambier, 1880 census)

Samuel and Filomena Pepe (Samuel and Minnie Piper, 1880 census)

Alessandro Pepe was born on April 27, 1849, in the comune of Ciorlano, Caserta Province. His parents were Antonio Pepe and Angiola Cardarelli. According to Alessandro's 1920 passport, he immigrated to the United States on May 26, 1874. By 1880, he was working on a railroad in Coalburg. There, he met and married a newly arrived Italian teenager, Maria Marino. They shared their Coalburg home with Alessandro's younger brother, Sabatino, who worked in a mine.

Alessandro and Maria had one child in Coalburg: Anthony, born in 1881. Two children were born in Youngstown: Louis in 1883 and Adella the following year. Later, the family moved to Niles, where Alessandro became a labor boss. In 1920, the seventy-one-year-old was still working, having attained the position of foreman. He died in 1928.

A second Pepe family resided within the village of Hubbard in 1880. They were Samuel, Filomena and their seven-month-old daughter, Millie. They lived in the home of Benjamin and Chancena Campia. Known as Jennie, Chancena was Samuel's older sister. She and Benjamin immigrated in 1874, while Samuel and Filomena arrived in 1880. By 1900, the two families had moved to Pittsburgh, where the Campias were living in a house owned by the Pepes.

Felice and Maria Assunta Menaldi
(Fileach and Saund C. Manalt, 1880 census)

On April 13, 1880, the SS *Castalia* arrived in New York. Among the passengers were three Menaldi men: Vincenzo, age forty-seven; Pasquale, twenty-nine; and Gaetano, fifty-three. The *Castalia* was a steam packet vessel operated by the Anchor Line, notorious in the 1880s for transporting Italian immigrants who were bound by onerous labor contracts under the control of bosses called *padrones*. Agents recruiting potential emigrants were most active in small towns in southern Italy, including Agnone.

Two months after their arrival, Pasquale, Vincenzo and Gaetano appeared on the Hubbard census of 1880, where they were listed as boarders in the Coalburg home of Felice and Assunta Menaldi. All four of the Menaldi men worked in the coal mines. As local coal production began to falter, Felice and Assunta moved to Youngstown in 1882, where records show that daughter Josephine was born on March 21. The couple returned to the city from a visit to Agnone, Italy on the SS *Normannia* on March 17, 1898. On the ship's manifest, Felice declared he had resided in Ohio between 1872 and 1896. Josephine's 1932 death certificate affirmed Agnone as the point of origin of the Menaldi family.

The document listed her parents' names as Felix Minaldi and Assunta Catelina, and it stated that Agnone was their place of birth.

Edward, the son of Felice and Assunta, worked at the Youngstown Macaroni Company and later operated his own grocery store at 214 North Hine Street.

Donatantonio and Christina Carosella
(Donath and Christina Carozel, 1880 census)

Donatantonio (Donato) and Christina Carosella were married in Agnone on September 4, 1879. Less than three months later, they came to the United States aboard the SS *Australia*, a steam packet vessel operated by the Anchor Line. He was listed as a coal miner on the 1880 census. The couple moved to Youngstown before 1900, and their children included Joseph, John, Antoinette, Philip and Carmela. Until Prohibition, Philip ran a saloon in Youngstown; afterward, he sold soft drinks until the early 1920s. By 1927, he was operating a bank, which was closed in April 1929, when he was arrested for embezzlement.

Donatantonio and Christina Carosella around 1900. *Robert and Carole Madeline.*

Michele and Filomena Di Giacomo
(Michael and Foloman Jackamo, 1880 census)

Michele Di Giacomo and Filomena Fabrizio were married in their hometown of Castiglione on May 5, 1870. The couple arrived in the United States aboard the SS *Tyrian* on June 5, 1877, accompanied by their seven-month-old daughter, Grazia (Mary Grace), and twelve-year-old son, Sabatino Di Giacomo. Within a short time, they joined the Italian enclave in Coalburg, where Sabatino rented a room in the Di Giacomo home and worked with Michele in the mines. Two other Di Giacomo men joined the household and were soon laboring beside Michele and Sabatino.

Michele and Filomena had two children born in Coalburg: Philip on July 2, 1879,[339] and Carmela on April 24, 1881.[340] A few years later, the couple moved the family back to Castiglione. On November 15, 1885, they registered their American-born daughter, Carmela, in the town's birth registry. Michele, who was illiterate, was accompanied by Giulio Cerulli and Luigi Conti, who witnessed the proceedings on Michele's behalf.[341]

Pasquale and Angela Di Giacomo
(Basqual and Anjaline Jackamo, 1880 census)

Pasquale Di Giacomo and Angela Meccia were married in Castiglione on February 15, 1868. By 1880, they were living in Coalburg, where the family name was anglicized as "Jackamo." Like the other Italian men in the coal camp, Pasquale was a miner. According to the 1880 census, a son, Mike (Michele), was born in Italy about 1877. Therefore, the family must have come to Coalburg between 1877 and 1880. Michele's birth and an 1874 manifest indicate that Pasquale may have made several trips between Italy and the United States. The couple had several more children, including Joseph, Sylvester, Mary and Philomena. A passenger list for the SS *Werra* shows the family returning from Carovilli to the United States on November 3, 1899. On the manifest, Pasquale declared they lived in Krebs, Indian Territory (Oklahoma), between 1885 and 1899. They eventually moved to the Italian settlement on Jackson Avenue in Hubbard, where Angela died on April 6, 1909. Pasquale died six months later, on October 28, 1909.

Pasquale and Angela weren't the only Coalburg residents who went to the Indian Territory. During the 1880s, the closure of the Mahoning Valley mines forced men to seek work elsewhere. Word reached Little Italy that miners were needed in the coal camp at Krebs, a few miles from McAlester. Several Coalburg families pulled up stakes and headed west to the rich prairie coalfields of the Indian Territory. Among them were Angelo and Domenica Di Giacomo.

Angelo and Domenica Di Giacomo

Angelo Di Giacomo was born in Castiglione in July 1865. On July 24, 1893, he married Domenica Scarduzzi at St. Patrick's Church in Hubbard. Their marriage was solemnized by Father Nicholas Drohan, who entered Angelo's surname as "Jackaman" in the church records. In 1936, Domenica filed an affidavit that claimed the correct spelling of her husband's surname was Di Giacomo. The affidavit held that Father Drohan was an "English speaking Pastor, [who] inserted the surname in the Church's record according to their phonetic pronunciation."[342]

Shortly after their wedding, the couple left for the Indian Territory, where Angelo found employment as a miner at the Ola station, three miles east of Wilburton. At sunrise on April 22, 1899, Angelo and two other Italians entered the Klondike bank in Ola. According to an official report filed by the mine owners with the Department of the Interior, the men stepped across a "dead line" made by the fire boss, who had detected the presence of gas. Unfortunately, an explosion took place, badly injuring Angelo and taking the life of one of his coworkers. Two days later, Angelo died at St. John's Hospital in South McAlester.[343] Domenica's son-in-law, Russell Benton, and granddaughter, Genevieve Wood, claimed that the mine owners had falsified the official report, covering up the failure of the fire boss to mark the location of the gas seep.[344]

Angelo Di Giacomo on the Fallen Miners Memorial Wall, McAlester, Oklahoma. *Steve DeFrange.*

Antonio and Filomena Rossi
(Anthony Jackamo and Faloman Domanic; Anthony was erroneously surnamed Jackamo on the 1880 census)

On February 19, 1874, the steamship *Nevada* arrived in New York carrying 112 passengers; nearly half of them were from Italy. Among the Italians were thirty-four-year-old Antonio Rossi and thirty-three-year-old Pasquale Giacomo. According to the 1880 census, Anthony (Antonio) Rossi lived with Pasquale and Angela Di Giacomo in Coalburg, so the 1874 manifest of the *Nevada* may be a record of the arrival of the two Coalburg residents. The census indicates that both Anthony and Pasquale were coal miners.

On October 13, 1879, a group of Italian immigrants entered the Port of New York aboard the steamship *Switzerland*, on which Angela Meccia and her children Sabatina, Rosa (probably Teresa Rosa), and Michele were passengers. Accompanying them were Anthony Rossi's wife, Filomena, and their daughter, Carmella.

When the mines began to close, the Rossi family moved two miles from Coalburg to the Italian enclave on Jackson Avenue in Hubbard, where daughter Carmella married Joseph Carano. In 1902, Joseph and Carmella purchased a building on the corner of Schofield Lane and North Main Street in Hubbard, which they converted into a saloon. It was across the street from Joe Madeline's saloon. Both men benefited from passengers using the streetcar station located in the Madeline building.

Anthony Rossi's 1921 obituary reported he was "one of the earliest Italian settlers to immigrate to this country."[345] The article further noted that he "came direct to Hubbard 48 years ago." This phrase might have meant that Anthony was brought straight from his ship to the mines, just as other Italians were brought directly from Castle Garden to Coalburg during the strike of 1873.

Donato and Maria Carmina Di Domenico
(D. Domnick, 1880 census)

Donato Di Domenico was born in 1842 in the small hamlet of Castiglione in what is today the province of Isernia. On September 30, 1879, he boarded the steamship *Switzerland* at Antwerp. His final destination was Hubbard. He was accompanied by two of his neighbors, Angela (Meccia) Di

Giacomo and Filomena (Di Dominicis) Rossi, who were going to Hubbard to join their husbands. Three farmers from Castiglione—Pietro Massaro, Fedelo Di Giacomo and Cosimo Massaro—also boarded the vessel. With their wives and children, they stopped briefly in Hubbard before continuing to Logan County, Arkansas, where they would resume their agricultural way of life. Thirty of Castiglione's residents embarked on the American-bound steamer that day; their departure was a major loss for so small a place.

Donato, who changed his name to Daniel Dominic when he arrived in Ohio, was digging in the Coalburg mines by the spring of 1880. His wife, Maria, remained in Italy with their three young children, Filomena, Lucia and Paolo. Four years later, they arrived in New York aboard the steamship *Burgundia* and were soon reunited with Daniel in Hubbard. Soon afterward, Lucia married Serafino Zarlenga, a native of Pietrabbondante, a small comune nestled in the hills of Isernia eight miles from Castiglione. The couple settled in Wooster, Ohio, where they joined Serafino's father, Pardo.

As the Coalburg mines closed, Daniel Dominic was forced to find work elsewhere. He moved his family to the Italian enclave on Jackson Avenue in Hubbard. His son, Paolo, known in Hubbard as Paul, married Mary Ferrando in 1895. He became a city councilman and a notary public, representing his fellow countrymen on their deeds and wills. By 1900, Paul was a grocer, and within a few years, he was a justice of the peace.

Arcangelo Di Giacomo and Genevieve Lumpp

Leopold Lumpp was born in 1833 in the Grand Duchy of Baden, an independent country until it joined the German Empire. In 1857, he migrated from Europe and settled in Hubbard, Ohio, where he opened a boot shop.[346] When the census was taken on June 7, 1880, it showed that he and his wife, Victoria, had seven children, among whom were a son, George, and a daughter, Genevieve. Two of their brothers, John and Joseph, worked in the coal beds. Through them, George and Genevieve became acquainted with an Italian miner named Arcangelo Di Giacomo.

According to Marco Antonelli, Di Giacomo was one of the Carovillesi brought to Hubbard during the 1873 miners' strike.[347] However, his time in Hubbard would be short-lived, since coal mining there was waning, and a wider world of opportunities was sapping the settlement of its more adventurous townsfolk. The seams were playing out, and some of the younger laborers were looking afar for other work—as far as the American South.

On October 30, 1875, the *Northern Ohio Journal*, a Painesville newspaper, reported the discovery of a vast coal bed beneath the northwest quadrant of Arkansas. It equaled the best Pittsburgh coals and soon found enthusiastic consumers along the Mississippi River. Diggings began in Johnson County on the north bank of the Arkansas River, where the community of Coal Hill was founded. Perhaps news of Arkansas's coal boom enticed Di Giacomo to pull up stakes, or maybe the impetus to "go west" was provided by his friend, George Lumpp. In an effort to populate the region with hard-working immigrants, the Little Rock & Fort Smith Railroad Company offered land to a group of Benedictine monks near the Arkansas River a dozen miles south of Coal Hill. They founded the St. Benedict Priory (now, the Subiaco Abbey) and soon began soliciting German Catholics to join their colony.[348] The son of a devout German Catholic, George Lumpp may have been drawn to Subiaco, Arkansas.

The railroad company advertised its land deal in newspapers across the country, including in the *Mahoning Vindicator* in April and May 1877. It boasted "prairie, timber and coal lands of the finest quality. Government homesteads free."

After a few years, Di Giacomo abandoned the coal pits of Trumbull County and journeyed to the hills of western Arkansas. But he did not go there alone. His parents and his sister, Eva, joined him at his home in Short Mountain Township, just four miles west of Subiaco. One more addition made the Di Giacomo household complete. On July 1, 1880, barely three weeks after her name was entered on the Hubbard census, Genevieve Lumpp exchanged wedding vows with Arcangelo Di Giacomo in Pulaski County, Arkansas.[349]

The former peasants from Carovilli were now earning a living by cultivating the soil. On September 10, 1890, the General Land Office of the United States endorsed Di Giacomo's claim to an eighty-acre homestead, declaring him a settler on the public domain.[350]

Although he was now a farmer, Di Giacomo hadn't lost interest in mining. He and George Lumpp, who had accompanied his sister to Arkansas, opened the first coal mine in Logan County in 1881.[351] Initially, they dug only enough coal for use in their blacksmith shop. Soon, their Lone Star Coal Company was supplying the community of Paris with fuel. "The coal was of premium quality, almost entirely free of impurities, smokeless, and unexcelled for heat-producing qualities."[352] When the county was linked by rail to industrial centers in the 1890s, the area's superior coal found ready buyers as far away as North Dakota. Mining in the county peaked in the

Lone Star Coal Mine, Paris, Arkansas, around 1890. *Ramona Black and the Logan County Historical Society.*

1920s, when dozens of shafts, employing two thousand men, produced eleven thousand tons annually.[353] The fine coal of Logan County, first mined by Di Giacomo and Lumpp, triggered the region's economic growth.

Aliodoro (Aliodore, Elidoro) Zarlenga

Marco Antonelli, who was interviewed by Charles Carr of the *Youngstown Daily Vindicator*, stated that one of the first Italians to enter the Trumbull County mines in 1873 was Aliodore Zarlenga, a native of Pietrabbondante.[354] In a community of so few inhabitants, it's tempting to identify him with Aliodoro Zarlenga, who was born there on August 5, 1833, the son of Domenico and Giovanna (Di Pasqua).

An additional corroboration is suggested by an entry in the 1880 census of Mantua Station, a hamlet about forty miles west of Hubbard. That enumeration listed a forty-eight-year-old stone mason from Pietrabbondante by the name of Elidoro Zarlinga.[355] When the miners' strike ended in

May 1873, many of the strikers returned to their old jobs. The Italian strikebreakers in Church Hill, who were hired under a two-month contract,[356] were reassigned to railroad work.[357] Elidoro may have been among them; his occupation as a stone mason may indicate that he built bridges for the railroad. The census reveals that a boarder in Elidoro's home also worked on the railroad, as did many of his neighbors.

Nicholas and Lujae Naach
(Nicholas and Lujae Naach, 1880 census)

Many of the Italians listed on the 1880 Hubbard census cannot be identified because their names are so badly misspelled. An example is the family of Nicholas and Lujae Naach. No other records exist for an Italian family with that surname, so we must assume their "real" name wasn't Naach but something phonetically similar.

According to the 1880 census, Nicholas Naach was born in 1850. The 1910 Denver census listed a Nicola Notch who was born in Italy around 1850 and immigrated about 1873. The Denver census agent was no better at spelling Italian names than his Hubbard counterpart; records show that Nicola Notch was Nicola Nuosci. He married Domenica Lucia Massaro in Castiglione on August 24, 1872, so it's likely "Lujae" from the 1880 census was Domenica Lucia. Records in Denver show that Nicola had a younger brother, Stephen, born about 1853. The February 19, 1874 arrival of the SS *Nevada* provides another possible link between Nicholas Naach and Nicola Nuosci. The manifest of the *Nevada* shows that just a few steps behind Antonio Rossi and Pasquale Giacomo were twenty-four-year-old Nicola Nuosci and twenty-one-year-old Stefano Nuosci.

The Likely First Birth of an Italian American in Coalburg

A Hubbard Township vital record shows that on February 5, 1874, Agnes Persuthig, wife of John Angelo, gave birth to a daughter, Sephronica Angelo. These are the registrants as they appear on page 340 of the *Ohio County Births, 1841–2003 for Trumbull County in the Birth Registers with Index 1867–1874, Volume 1.*

The surname Angelo can be found in Italy as well as De Angelo and D'Angelo. If Angelo is an Italian name, then this child could be the earliest

Birth of Sephronica Angelo in Hubbard, February 5, 1874. *Trumbull County Courthouse.*

born to Italian immigrants in Trumbull County. In the early 1870s, Trumbull County agents did not yet have experience with Italian names. If the Angelos were Italians, it is likely that the mother's maiden name, Persuthig, and the child's first name, Sephronica, were an agent's attempts to write names spoken in what was probably a foreign tongue. It is also possible that Sephronica was a misspelling of the Italian name Serafina

In 1874, Coalburg didn't have its own section in the birth registers, so an infant born there would have been recorded as having been born in Hubbard Township, as was the case for Sephronica. Working backward, the date of her birth places her conception no earlier than late April 1873. The first large group of Italian immigrants in the Mahoning Valley was brought to Coalburg on March 19, 1873, so it's possible Sephronica's parents were among them.

Unfortunately, this birth record is the only known trace left by the Angelo family. Whether they moved to another part of the United States or returned to their country of origin is unknown. The only facts in our possession are the birth date and birthplace of the child, the questionable spelling of her mother's last name and the Latin origin of their surname. Everything else is pure speculation.

The Earliest Known Document for an Italian Resident of Hubbard Township

On July 2, 1873, a marriage was performed in Hubbard Township by Alexander King, a justice of the peace.[358] The bride was Josephine Zaliski, who may have been of German, Polish or Russian descent. According to the court document, her new husband was Jacomo Silvastoro.

The marriage license was signed by Albert Yeomans, a probate judge in Trumbull County.[359] Born in Kinsman, Ohio, Albert was probably unfamiliar with the foreign languages spoken by the immigrants in his court. If so, "Jacomo" could have been his attempt to spell the Italian name Giacomo. In 1873, the majority of the newly arrived Italians in Trumbull

County could not speak English, and a great number were illiterate. In these circumstances, "Silvastoro" could have been a misspelling of the groom's surname. Silvestro and Silvestri are common names in the area around Naples, which was the point of origin for many of the immigrants brought to the mines of Trumbull County.

At face value, the record indicates the wedding of an Italian and a woman of Eastern European ancestry. At a time when immigrants married almost exclusively within their ethnic communities, it seems unlikely that such a marriage could have taken place. However, the dangers in the mines forged a brotherhood among men of all races. By the summer of 1873, friendships may have formed between the Italians and Eastern Europeans who were working side by side in the pits. A wedding between mining families of different ethnicities seems to be borne out by these records. If so, the marriage record is the earliest known document for an Italian in Hubbard Township, registered less than four months after the importation of the Italian immigrants to the Coalburg mines.

OBSCURITY

Drawn by the prospect of jobs in Coalburg, many Italians passed through Hubbard Township during the 1870s and 1880s. Those who entered the mines labored in obscurity, leaving little or no trace of their presence. In 1921, a fire destroyed most of the 1890 federal census records in Washington, D.C. More recently, a flood caused the loss of many parish documents at St. Patrick's Church in Hubbard.

Only from fragmentary, fleeting reports can the lives of early immigrants be glimpsed. Frequently in the late 1800s, government agents had difficulty accurately spelling the sounds when illiterate immigrants spoke their names. Often, as in the cases of miners Giovanni Chiesa (John Church) and Pasquale Jackamo (Di Giacomo), newcomers from Italy opted for Anglicized names, thereby leaving their birth names lost to posterity.

Despite these obstacles to research, the Coalburg Italians do occasionally appear in the historical record. Giuseppe Santangelo was among the Italian replacement miners brought to Trumbull County in the spring of 1873. In May, he was injured in a blasting procedure at a mine operated by the Mahoning Coal Company in Coalburg. His right leg was amputated to forestall an infection, but he died from the injury on May 16, 1873.[360]

On May 22, 1877, two men were hurt when an accumulation of firedamp exploded in a Coalburg mine. Firedamp, a mixture of methane and other flammable gases, was a constant threat to miners. The injured men were John Christofery and John G. Garabalda.[361] It's possible that "Garabalda" was a misspelling of Garibaldi or Garibaldo. According to the January 5, 1925 edition of the *Youngstown Vindicator*, Giovanni Cristoforo (John Christofery) was one of the Italians brought to Coalburg as a strikebreaker on March 19, 1873. Located beneath Coalburg's northwestern edge, the passages of the Stewart Coal Bank twisted like the tentacles of a subterranean monster. On January 4, 1877, Nicolas Salvo was digging in one of its tunnels when a mass of rocks in the ceiling fell and killed him. Six months later and a half-mile away, Dominic and Vincenzo Santangelo were working together in Mine Number 3, a pit operated by the Mahoning Coal Company, when the roof collapsed, killing them instantly.[362] This was the same mine where John Turrill, Thomas Bowen and the Miller brothers had been trapped for a week by floodwaters in July 1865.[363]

Giovanni Santangelo was an immigrant from the small town of Pietrabbondante, in what is now the province of Isernia. He was among the group of Italians imported to Coalburg in March 1873.[364] He married Agnes Gelynski in Hubbard on December 14, 1878, after which they both disappear from the archival records.[365]

For some immigrants, Coalburg was a way station. For others it became a permanent residence. But for one young traveler bound for the little mining community, Coalburg may have remained out of reach.

On March 12, 1880, a group of Italian immigrants arrived in New York aboard the steamer *India*. Among them was a seven-year-old boy named Leonardo Cianfrani. He had been accompanied by his father at the outset of his journey, but just before the ship sailed, Leonardo's father mysteriously vanished, leaving the boy to embark alone or in the company of relatives. Upon arriving at Castle Garden, the distraught boy told an interpreter that he had an uncle living in Coalburg. Whether the boy and his uncle were reunited, or whether he was returned to Italy, remains unknown.

EPILOGUE

The breaking of the miners' strike of 1873 accomplished two things, one intentional and the other unforeseen. The owners achieved their goal of reopening their mines by importing African Americans and immigrants, among whom the Italian recruits figured largely. It also spurred an unprecedented flood of arrivals from Italy to the Mahoning Valley. Those first, pioneering Italians blazed a trail that others soon followed. As strikebreakers in the mines, and later as employees of the railroads, they set an example for their fellow countrymen back in the struggling villages of southern Italy. There was, indeed, an American market for Italian labor. Consequently, more *paesani* began arriving in the Mahoning Valley hungry for work. They were also, quite literally, starving.

> *At a miners' boarding house, at Coalburg, at which nine boarders were kept, those nine ate, in one week, 140 pounds meat, 69 loaves bread, 180 eggs, 18 pounds ham, 22 pounds sugar, 5 pounds rice, 3 bushels potatoes, 100 pickles, washing all this down with 21 pounds of coffee. These boarders were of the imported miners from New York. It is probable, from the foregoing exhibit, that they never had enough to eat, before, in all their lives.*[366]

Eager to join their compatriots in the New World, almost nine thousand Italians entered the United States in 1873, more than double the number who had come during the previous year.[367] Within a few months, thousands of them migrated to industrial centers where captains of local industries were eager to hire them. Their seeming acquiescence to work as strikebreakers or for low wages pleased their employers but concerned their American counterparts. Their sudden appearance in the workplace caused Americans to take stock of the newcomers:

> *Where they* [Italians] *have already been employed in the neighborhood of Youngstown, the other workmen at first resisted their importation with threats and blows, and failing to intimidate them, endeavored to win them from their employers over to the Union, or induce them to go back to New York. These efforts though attended with some success at first, ultimately failed, and the Italians to-day, we believe, are employed in some of the mines near Youngstown. The testimony that comes from other places, however, is that these Italians are neither lazy, worthless or dirty. They are generally from the country districts of Italy, who, only within two years, have found out the fact that the United States is a good country to emigrate to, and are coming every year in increasing numbers. They are said to be intelligent, honest and industrious, and what is of full as much account, to*

make orderly, peaceable, and sober citizens. If this is so they are a valuable acquisition to our population, and should be welcomed not only by our operators, but by the workmen with whom they will henceforth labor.[368]

The process of integration took decades and saw ups and downs, as in the Johnson Reed Act restrictions on non-Nordic immigration and the brief but shameful "alien enemy" status of World War II. Still, Italians now make their presence felt in all walks of life and social classes in the Mahoning Valley and throughout the United States. Old, racialized descriptions and anti-Catholic bias directed at Italian Americans have largely disappeared. Yet a close reading of American history reminds us that the mixture of ethnic differences and competition for work, as revealed in *Coal War in the Mahoning Valley*, remains a volatile and dangerous social lever in the hands of the powerful.

INACCURACIES IN THE *YOUNGSTOWN VINDICATOR*

Four articles in the *Youngstown Vindicator* introduced errors about the origin of Youngstown's Italian American community. These have persisted to the present day. On July 10, 1910, Charles Carr penned a local history piece, "Tales of the City's Industries—The First Strikebreakers in Youngstown." Among other things, the *Vindicator* reporter described how two delegations of laborers were imported to fill local mines abandoned by strikers. Carr explained that the strike began when miners rejected a pay cut from $1.10 to 90¢ per ton, proposed in the fall of 1871. He stated that mine owners brought replacement workers to Youngstown in the "winter of 1872." In fact, contemporary newspapers remarked that miners' wages didn't reach $1.10 until November 1872.[369] It wasn't until the spring of 1873 that the press reported on the introduction of Italian strikebreakers to the Mahoning Valley. It's an established fact that the miners' strike did not begin until January 1, 1873.

More than forty years later, Ann Przelomski wrote a story for the April 29, 1951 edition of the *Youngstown Vindicator* titled "Sons of Sunny Italy Largest Unit Here." She chronicled the sequence of events that led from the miners' strike to the establishment of the city's large Italian population. She erroneously claimed that Italians were introduced to Mahoning Valley mines early in 1872, when a labor contractor recruited the immigrants in New York and brought them to Ohio to act as strikebreakers. In reality, the Mahoning Valley saw no widespread coal miners' strike that year. The April 25, 1873 *Canton Repository and Republican* reported the dispatch of a

Youngstown labor contractor to Castle Garden in March 1873 to recruit Italian immigrants for the Mahoning Coal Company. The year before, there simply was no need for hundreds of strikebreakers to keep mines open in the Mahoning Valley.

Przelomski also claimed that, when the foreigners were brought to the company's Coalburg mines, newspaperman A.D. Fassett galloped into the encampment on a horse to obstruct them.[370] This claim is at variance with contemporary newspaper coverage. The March 28, 1873 *Mahoning Vindicator* reported that Fassett rode to Coalburg on a train. Written a week after the importation of the Italians, the story represented a firsthand account of the affair, while Przelomski's article wasn't composed until seventy-eight years later.

According to Przelomski, Stefano Colucci arrived in the United States in 1871. Yet Joseph G. Butler Jr. wrote that Colucci immigrated on September 12, 1872, and that he was later hired to work in a Coalburg mine in the spring of 1873.[371] Butler may have known Colucci personally, but both were deceased by the time Przelomski published her article in 1951. It's much more likely that Butler, a contemporary of Colucci, would have had a more accurate date for the Italian's immigration. Significantly, several historic records weigh heavily against the date of 1871: Colucci's 1905 U.S. passport application and the federal censuses of 1900, 1920 and 1930. In all four, he attests to 1872 as the year of his immigration to the United States.

In 1924 and 1925, the *Youngstown Vindicator* published a series of articles titled "Knowing Youngstown" that included more than a hundred stories covering local topics, with themes as wide-ranging as fossils, railroads and the iron industry. Early in January 1925, the *Youngstown Vindicator* featured two segments about the origin of Youngstown's Italian community. The pair of stories incorrectly ascribed 1872 as the year of the first Italian settlement in the Mahoning Valley. Installment 81 of the series, "The Italians in Youngstown," carries I. Vagnozzi's byline of January 3, 1925. Among other things, he stated that the first Italians appeared in Youngstown in May 1872. He further asserted that the Morris brothers introduced 105 Italian immigrants to their Church Hill collieries, and that their original settlement was in Brier Hill. There is no evidence to corroborate Vagnozzi's claim for the arrival of a large group of Italians in 1872. Such an event would have been reported on the front pages of area newspapers, since the census of 1870 failed to account for a single Italian in Mahoning County and only 1 in nearby Vienna Township, Trumbull County.

Charles Carr's story, "More About Youngstown's Italians," was the eighty-second installment of the "Knowing Youngstown" series and appeared in the *Vindicator* on January 5, 1925. He (incorrectly) claimed the labor contractor who was sent to New York brought newly arrived Italian immigrants to Youngstown in 1872. Howard Charles Aley published the same inaccuracies in his book, *A Heritage to Share: The Bicentennial History of Youngstown and Mahoning County, Ohio, from Prehistoric Times to the National Bicentennial Year.* A scrutiny of the chapter "First Italian Immigrants Reached Mahoning County in 1871" demonstrates that he paraphrased Przelomski's 1951 article, thereby preserving her errors.[372]

There were no strikes in the greater Youngstown area settled with the introduction of outside laborers during the period that Carr and others suggest as dates for the coming of the Italians. If newcomers from Italy had worked as general labor or as miners, the appearance of foreign speaking, destitute Italian Catholics would have created front-page news. Only in March 1873 do contemporary press reports begin citing the arrival of Italians to the area.

COALBURG ON GOVERNMENT DOCUMENTS

Coalburg was well known from Youngstown to Cleveland and Chicago during the 1860s and 1870s, but few official documents attest to its existence. The first time the community was named in a document occurred when the "Coalburgh" Post Office was established on March 27, 1867. On December 1, 1894, the name of the facility was changed to the Coalburg Post Office.[373] It was finally closed on February 15, 1913.[374]

Coalburg's name appeared on a census for the first time when it was listed as an "unincorporated place" in the heading of the 1940 federal census.[375]

APPENDIX 3

DATA FOR SELECT MINES IN CHURCH HILL AND COALBURG

In his study *Investigation and Inventory of Abandoned Underground Mines in Columbiana, Mahoning, and Trumbull Counties, Ohio: Data Sheets for Trumbull County* (Columbus: Department of Natural Resources, 1980), Douglas L. Crowell suggested that the Eureka mine was one of the first mines in Hubbard Township. An earlier report, published in the *Hubbard News*, stated the Love Bank was the first mine opened in the area.[376]

Name	Active Years	Peak Output	Notes
Centennial	1876 - ?		workd by 342 men in 1874
Chinee	1865 - ?		
Church Hill #1	1864? - 1886		large mine; connects to Centennial Shaft
Church Hill #2	1880 - 1886		serviced by narrow-gauge steam engine
High Tone			full of horsebacks; also known as Blaine
Hood	1871 - 1877		a large mine
Kline	1867 - 1886	250 tons/day	600,000 tons removed by 1883
Mahoning No. 9	1880 - 1885		thirty acres of coal removed
Niles	? - 1897		connects to Church Hill mine
Sodom	1871 - 1877	200 tons/day	also known as McCurdy
Taylor/Pumpkin	1868 - 1885		a small mine

Select Church Hill coal mines. *Information from Douglas Crowell,* Investigation and Inventory of Abandoned Underground Mines in Columbiana, Mahoning and Trumbull Counties, Ohio *(Columbus: Department of Natural Resources, 1980).*

APPENDIX 3

Name	Active Years	Peak Output	Notes
Applegate	1871 - 1883	300 tons/day	connects to Love/Lane mine
Burnett Bank	1863 - 1883	450 tons/day	large railroad mine; burnt by arson, 1875
California			
Eureka	? - 1870		one of the first mines in the Township
Long	1864 - 1877	150 tons/day	
Love	1857 - ?		probably the first mine in the Township
Love/Lane	1872 - 1883	400 tons/day	connects with Applegate Mine
Mahoning No. 1	? - 1882		total yield of 500,000 tons
Mahoning No. 3	<1865 - 1883	400 tons/day	Charles Herbert, manager in 1875
Mahoning No. 4			
Mahoning No. 8	1880 - 1883		connects to Mahoning No. 3
New California	1882 - 1883		William Parker, mine boss
Stewart	1870? - 1877?	300 tons/day	a large operation

Select Coalburg coal mines. *Information from Douglas Crowell,* Investigation and Inventory of Abandoned Underground Mines in Columbiana, Mahoning and Trumbull Counties, Ohio *(Columbus: Department of Natural Resources, 1980).*

THE BEGINNING OF THE MASSIVE IMMIGRATION OF DESTITUTE ITALIANS

The first large-scale arrivals of poor Italian immigrants occurred in the fall of 1872. In September 1872, the *New York Herald* noted, without alarm or other negative comment, an increase in immigration from Italy during June of that year compared to June of the previous year.[377] In November 1872, three completely unrelated factors sparked a sudden increase in Italian immigration to the United States. The worsening economic situation in southern Italy and the increasing affordability of oceanic transportation made emigration a viable option for some. But a deception perpetrated on the lower classes prompted a dramatic surge of departures. Incredibly, many of the Italians arrived in New York in a state of financial ruin.

One of the first groups of destitute Italians arrived at the Port of New York on November 18, 1872, aboard the steamship *Holland*. This is the story of their sojourn.

Early in the autumn of that year, circulars printed in Genoa began appearing in villages throughout southern Italy. The publications advertised an abundance of rich farmland and plentiful jobs in Argentina.[378] According to the circulars, Italians who wished to immigrate there could receive assistance from the Colonization Society, an agency based in the French port of Le Havre. Agents representing the society offered a financial plan to those who couldn't afford to pay for the transatlantic passage. The plan required customers to mortgage their property in exchange for the steamship fare. If the loan, including 15-percent interest, was not repaid within twelve months, the mortgage would revert to the agency.[379] In October 1872, nearly three hundred Italian peasants agreed to these terms in exchange for transportation to Argentina on the SS *Holland*. They sold or mortgaged all their possessions and began the first stage of their journey, the poorest of them on foot.[380] On October 28, 1872, they gathered in Naples and were greeted by agents representing the Colonization Society, who loaded them onto a steamer bound for Marseille.[381] From there, the emigrants were taken by train to Le Havre. When they arrived at the port, they were told the steamer for Buenos Aires was delayed, but another ship could take them to New York, where they would be transferred to Argentina. The agents booked them onto the steamship *Holland* and promised them a warm welcome by their representatives in the United States. The immigrants reached the Port of New York on November 18, 1872, and, clutching letters of introduction, hurried to the office of the Commissioners of Emigration. The travelers were surprised that none of the officials had ever heard of the Colonization Society.[382] The immigrants had been swindled. Undaunted, the anxious newcomers sat down to await the arrival of the agents who had promised to meet them. They waited through the long afternoon and far into the night, but nobody ever came. The final blow fell when officials of the National Line, the operator of the *Holland*, denied any knowledge of the fraud.[383] Unbelievably, all the agents implicated in the swindle were authorized by the government of Italy.[384]

The leaders of the Italian Society of New York believed the Colonization Society was "organized, or at least connived at, by the Italian government."[385] Robert Prati, the president of the Italian Society, said Ferdinando De Luca, the Italian consul in New York, and the Italian government were "accomplices" in the swindling operation.[386] The perpetrators, operating beyond the reach of the U.S. government, were so successful they struck again. Six weeks after the arrival of the *Holland*, the steamship *Erin* docked in New York. The voyage of the *Erin* bore the hallmarks of the swindlers: impoverished Italians from southern Italy who were booked on a National Line vessel at Le Havre.

Between November 1872 and January 1873, several other transatlantic voyages of National Line ships followed the same pattern. The steamship *Denmark* left London on October 19, 1872, and arrived in New York on November 8 after boarding additional passengers at Le Havre on October 23.[387] On December 10, 1872, a group of poor Italians arrived in New York aboard the *Queen*.[388] More destitute Italians, also from the Naples area, arrived in New York on the steamship *Denmark* on January 5, 1873.[389]

The ship left London on December 13 and picked up additional passengers at Le Havre on December 16. Of the 281 passengers it carried, 250 were half-starved Italians.[390]

Hordes of penniless Italians bearing almost no possessions were pouring into the United States. The question was: who paid for the passage?

> *Pauper Italian immigrants are arriving at New York in such numbers as to give rise to the suspicion that the Italian government are systematically shipping the lazzaroni to this country. Those who have landed are reported as almost destitute of all things, to look half starved, and generally in such condition as to suggest doubts as to their having paid their own passage.*[391]

Common factors show the same swindlers perpetrated the frauds on the steamships *Holland* and *Erin*. In both incidents, passengers reported that shipping agents from Genoa, Naples and Turin claimed that fabulous fortunes awaited them in the Americas.[392] Italians travelling on both ships believed Buenos Aires was their final destination.[393] The National Line operated both ships, and the two voyages began at Le Havre. Most of the passengers on both vessels were too poor to have paid for their fares. The Italians on the *Holland* were destitute, and many of the Italian passengers on the *Erin* "were not able to pay their own passage."[394]

Finally, at least two of the fraudulent shipping agents booked passengers on both ships. Felix Carbone, Antonio Grottola, Alfonso Bojano, Michele Cerello and Fedele Garupolo, all passengers on the *Holland*, testified that the agents responsible for posting the circulars and arranging the mortgage deals were "Roches Padre & Figlio, Turin;" where "Padre & Figlio" is translated as "Father & Son."[395] Michele De Philipo, a passenger on the *Erin*, said his contacts were "the agents of Rochas, father and son."[396]

DESCENT INTO HUBBARD TOWNSHIP MINES

These are firsthand descriptions of descents into two mines in Hubbard Township. The first was at the Burnett Bank, on the eastern edge of Coalburg. The story, "Fossil Forests: Visit to the Great Coal Region of the Mahoning Valley," was published in the *Chicago Republican* on April 6, 1868:

INTO THE DEPTHS

Here it is our good fortune to become acquainted with Mr. Chauncey H. Andrews, of the firm Andrews, Hitchcock & Co., foremost among the coal kings, and well known to be the largest operators in Brier Hill coal in the country.

Seated behind a pair of splendid bays, we accompany Mr. Andrews six or seven miles in the direction of the main line of this road, our destination being the celebrated "Burnett Bank," with whose valuable qualities Chicago has long been acquainted. A stranger, perhaps, would no more suspect one of the great coal monarchs of the country in the unobtrusive gentleman we are accompanying, than the existence of great mineral wealth under the modest looking hills of this apparently rich agricultural region….

"Burnett Bank" is only one of Messrs. Andrews, Hitchcock & Co.'s numerous coal mines. It is a hill of moderate elevation, and with gently sloping sides, but covering a large extent of surface, and bearing a generous growth of timber. As we drive along a well-beaten road winding among the trees, it seems rather a portion of some picturesque park than the heart of a

great coal region. Just at the verge of the crown of the hill we come upon an odd looking structure, smoke begrimed, and open like a saw-mill. We are at the entrance of our coal mine.

A number of brawny fellows are at work here, concerning whom, judging from their faces, there is no prejudice of color. On one side, and somewhat below this structure, is a workman of more powerful mold, to whose energy clouds of steam and smoke testify. On another side, and still lower down but close to and almost beneath the building, is a branch of the "Hubbard Branch" and a long train of cars partially loaded with coal. In the rear, and a little further toward the top of the hill is a dark and gloomy chasm pitching at an angle of thirty degrees into the hill "Rock-ribbed and ancient as the sun" and down this opening another and smaller railway. One learns the uses of things here without asking many questions; one has only to give play to imagination. A bell attached to a wire running into the black depths suddenly tinkles as though just then "Kobold stirred himself" and the great engine, understanding it perfectly, begins to groan and puff; a rumble as though a small earthquake had awakened, succeeds, and presently a train of cars, piled with glistening masses of black diamonds, emerges from the chasm and rolls into the building. We examine with interest this latest exportation from the realms of darkness. On the great chunks of coal of each car are queer looking hieroglyphics, faintly resembling numbers. Perhaps they are the accounts which his majesty below keeps with the mortals of the upper air. Not just that—"it is the number of the room," and we straightway learn that there are, if not mansions, at least "rooms" below, and that they are numbered, and that the occupant of each room inscribes the number thereof upon the coal he digs from it. After seeing each car run upon scales and weighed, and then run upon another contrivance, which tips up and startles the visitor by nearly reversing itself, and discharging the coal into the railroad cars below, we make ready to go into the depths.

To effect this, we do not exactly exchange clothing, like Sir Matthew Hale and the miller, but borrow divers articles of apparel from men of a more dingy hue, and covered with a very greasy tile and provided with a lamp of Lilliputian dimensions which a Gnome just emerged unhooks from his head-gear for us, with careful steps and slow we begin our "Descensus Averni." At the depth of eighty or one hundred feet, we find ourselves, with the exception of the faint glimmer of the tiny lamps, in not "outer" darkness but darkness condensed, if such were possible, by the weight of hundreds of thousands of tons of rock and earth. An iron pipe extends along the side of the slope, and through it is lifted the water that would otherwise flood the mine. At the foot of the slope begins the main entry, here wide enough for several tracks, and mules and drivers, and loaded cars waiting to go up to daylight, and empty cars which have just returned therefrom all mixed and crowded in obscurity, somewhat add to the confusion of an already tolerably blind imagination. In some mysterious way we become seated in a car upon a tolerably clean board mysteriously provided. A tremendous jerk from some unseen cause which quite upsets the fleshy vessel of our dignity, and we are conscious of spinning rapidly along in the darkness. There is a splashing of water, but no water is visible; a voice somewhere in the obscurity shouts "look out for your head." It thereupon occurs, as our head comes in violent contact with the immensely hard rock above, that this vain warning might have been meant for us. Peering into the gloom ahead, we presently descry our locomotive power—the mule; his ears, too, were rubbing against the slate above, and he worked them backwards and forwards as if we were all one huge snail, of which he was the intelligent head, and his ears the antennae with which he felt his way along. But the mule knew what he was about, and so did his driver, who clung to the rear of our car of night, and shouted ghostly exhortations to our long-eared locomotive.

Presently we hold the tiny rush-light so as to examine the roof of the wonderful passage we were threading under the hills. What a sight! Imagination involuntarily goes back into antediluvian centuries! The dark shale close to our eyes is a vast herbarium of stone, and the impressions of the plants of the carboniferous period are as distinct as if crystalized from darkness by the ancient frost-king, or carved from ebony with fairy chisels. The names of the plants represented by these wonderful forms, our knowledge of preadamite [sic] biology is too imperfect to give—but it was marvelous to think that they thrived and flourished when the world was young, to furnish the human race with power.

We alight, and assuming a position in which the upper half of our body forms a right angle with the remainder, enter a "room"—a place in itself and its relations more remarkable than any other that is occupied by our varied industries. We are a good mile from the nearest daylight in a "black hole," a dozen yards square or less, in which we cannot stand erect, the entire altitude being only about four and a half feet. The fire-fly lamps show on every side solid glistening masses of the finest coal in the world. A brawny, straight-haired colored gentleman, with a lamp attached to his leathern cap, is reclining on his side, and vigorously cutting with a sharp pick-axe a deep gash in the solid coal wall near the level of the floor. This is "bearing-in," and presently with wedges or gunpowder, or with his pick, he will bring down great masses which he will pile upon his car ready for transportation to daylight. Judging from the sensations in our agonized spinal column, everybody must work here at a terrible disadvantage. Think of spending the working hours of a lifetime with one's body bent in the shape of a carpenter's square!

The miner with whom we conversed was intelligent, took pride in his occupation, fully understood the vast industrial importance of the material he was producing, and gaily left his work to hunt for us specimens of vegetable impressions in pieces of slate and coal. No philosophy, however, could prevent our deep commiseration for the monotonous fate to which one man in the mine voluntarily condemns himself. An incomprehensible mortal has done this work in utter darkness and solitude for years, working twelve hours a day, and, strange to tell, retaining a mental condition of cheerful sanity.

The second report, "The Mining Industry—Down in a Coal Mine," appeared in the *Cleveland Leader* on July 7, 1879:

Through the courtesy of Mr. D.H. Williams, one of the owners and the superintendent of the Hubbard mines, I had the pleasure of making the descent of a coal mine this afternoon. Placing myself upon the platform of an elevator in company with a miner, the word was given and we were at once lowered ninety feet, where the elevator suddenly halted. Stepping off into a mixture of water and clay, I crept along through a passage about two and a half or three feet high, for about five minutes, when the point was reached where a miner was delving into the coal. It was hard enough to crawl through such a passage and remain there for a few minutes, but to work there day after day is a hardship which few are able to appreciate. The miner lay on his side where he pecked away at the hard coal bank from morning until night, only emerging for dinner. Of course he was glad to get the work, and he had nothing but words of commendation for Mr. Williams, the superintendent. In another part of the mine was a lad fifteen years of age, his face as black as a crow, who told me, with a cheerful laugh, that he earned from fifty to sixty cents per day. The men whom I saw in this mine were hardy and robust, accustomed to their work, and pleased with it provided they can get enough of it.

The greatest complaint among the men employed in some mines in this neighborhood, is that they are compelled to expend their wages at a store owned by the company for which they work. They receive in payment pieces of scrip which are good only at one store. The result is that they are compelled to pay from five to fifteen percent more for what they buy than the same goods could be bought for elsewhere.

APPENDIX 6

"A PITTSBURGHER'S OPINION OF THE STRIKE"

What follows is a detailed report of the recruitment and transportation of the immigrants who were brought to Coalburg in March 1873. This account was published on April 25, 1873, in the *Canton Repository and Republican.*

> *The Pittsburgh Evening Leader sent a reporter into the Mahoning Valley to learn the truth concerning the existing strike and not rely on "specials" from the operators, as the Commercial and others do, and the following is extracted from the Leader's reports.*
>
> *The Mahoning Coal Company—especially obnoxious to the strikers—met to consider the situation, and after discussion, it was resolved that the best thing the company could do, would be to*

IMPORT IMPECUNIOUS ITALIANS

On the 18ᵗʰ of March Mr. Sanford arrived in New York, and proceeding to the commissioners of emigration, he informed them of his mission. It will be remembered that the large number of destitute Italians, about whose arrival there was such universal indignation manifested last winter, still remained in New York. They were in quarters on Wards island, and were a dead loss to the commissioners, being supplied at the public expense. Mr. Sanford made his arrangements to procure some of them for the Mahoning Coal Company, and accordingly the necessary formalities were concluded.

The following is a report of the experience of the Italians as given to our reporter by the interpreter, Mr. Behringer.

"Mr. Sanford made a verbal agreement that we were to work in a coal bank. The Italians had no idea that they would have to go below; in fact they did not understand fully what they were hired for. The Germans in the party had some knowledge of what coal mining is, but did not think it was as hard work as it is. My first impulse was to ask Mr. Sanford if there was a strike. My reasons for so doing were because I was suspicious, that it was queer that he should come all the way here to hire 250 men to work in a coal bank. He said

'It Is All Right'

"that there was no trouble whatever, that he wanted to commence and dig a new bank. He said the miners who were here were all working in the old bank, and we would be safe from any trouble. When [we] arrived at Leavittsburg some of the miners came aboard and said there would be trouble, as there was a strike here. This was the first we heard of any fuss, so we asked Mr. Sanford again, and he said there was no trouble at all. We were to have nice houses and everything in first class style, but when we got to Coalburg we found it was not so. We were put into unfurnished houses, and after a while two wagons came up with pots and pans for cooking but no furniture.

"We were given something to eat, each one getting a loaf of bread and an ounce of cheese for supper, and coffee and sugar were given in bulk to us to cook. Each man went to the company's office and got a blanket, and the next morning we went to work. Then some of the miners came up and told us that if we had some feelings for poor men we would stop work, as it was depriving them of a day's work we staying here. I told them as spokesman for the party, that I could guarantee for the Germans present, that we would not stay if it were doing them an injury. At a meeting the miners gave us $342 to pay our expenses away and leave for good."

On Thursday night the miners visited the mines at Coalburg in force, and significantly motioned to the Italians that they were in danger. This was done by drawing the fore finger across the throat when a general panic took place among the colonists. They were greatly alarmed, and that night the entire crowd left Coalburg and came to Youngstown, walking along the railroad track. Next morning they were found scattered *in groups around town, frightened and friendless, their position was to be regretted, and they were generally commiserated. A number of them gathered at the depot, and the Mahoning Coal Company managed to induce fifty of the crowd to return to work. The others were taken in charge by the strikers, and taken to Puddler's hall, where they were kept locked up until Sunday evening.*

Sunday Operations

The Sabbath was a busy one with both parties. It was apprehended by the operators that an attack would be made by the strikers on the Mahoning company's works in Coalburg, and on Sunday morning a large crowd of citizens went to that point from Youngstown. A guard had been sent there the night before, and they were determined to protect the Italians from violence. On the same train which conveyed the citizens was Mr. Fassett, the editor of the Miner and Manufacturer, and a prominent friend of the miners in their strike. On their arrival at the works, Mr. Fassett went up in the rear of the party of Youngstown people.

An Editor's Troubles

He was soon after ordered away by Mr. Brown of the Mahoning Coal Company, and obeyed, going on, as he believed, the highway. The following is his own language as to what followed: "I stood talking with a gentleman, When Dick Brown came up and grabbed me by the arm with both hands and gave me a jerk, saying, 'You have been ordered to leave here. Now get off.' I was about to answer I supposed I was on the highway when I was grabbed by the throat and arm by Tom and Richard Brown, who began choking me all they could. I tried to get loose and in doing so I was caught by four others, who all grabbed for my throat, when I thought they wanted to kill me and wanted me to resist enough to justify them in so doing, so I gave up, and they choked me until I became insensible. My first recollections were of a crowd of about a dozen with Tom Brown shaking his fist and saying 'Shall I kill you?' I called for help and was soon after released by all except the Browns, who still had hold of my throat and arms, and walked me about ten rods, and giving me a shove, let me go. I went to Coalburg, got a buggy, came home and made information against them. They gave bail."

Appendix 6

Operations in Town

On the same night, Sunday, the Mayor of Youngstown, with a posse of police and several operators, went to the hall and demanded that it be opened to see if there was any disease among the men who were kept there by the miners. Entrance was at first refused, but finally the mayor, police and operators were admitted, and a speech was made by some of the leading men to the Italians. They were invited to return to the works and promised ample protection. This was evidently producing some impression upon the Italians and the operators left. The miners then came to the conclusion that nothing but quick work would save them.

At 1 o'clock on Monday morning the miners got all the Italians and Germans they could, and while the operators were unsuspicious that anything was going on, the entire lot of imported laborers were walked to Girard and shipped by rail to Garrettsville, where work had been procured for them on a railroad. The operators on finding out the trick played on them were soon actively at work, and agents were sent after the wanderers, and some of them induced to return.

An Operator Interviewed

Our reporter called on Mr. Powers, one of the leading operators and of the Powers coal company, and the following is the interview which took place.
Rep.—Mr. Powers, do the operators propose trying to arrange this affair, will they make any concessions?
Mr. P.—No sir, none whatever.
Rep.—What is the object of the operators?
Mr. P.—To protect our interests, to burst the Miners' Union, and see that no man in sympathy with them, or who has made threats, gets employment.
Rep.—Are the operators agreed on this plan?
Mr. P.—Yes sir, to a unit.
Rep.—Do you propose to import any more foreign laborers?
Mr. P.—Yes sir, there are 300 more coming right away.
Rep.—Do you apprehend any serious violence?
Mr. P.—Not much, the strikers know better.
Rep.—How are the colored men getting along?
Mr. P.—Excellently. They give us all the satisfaction possible and so do the Italians. We will carry things with a bold front and crush opposition.

Appendix 6

The Present State of the Strike

The miners, several of whom our reporter interviewed, express confidence in their ability to carry their point. They all deny that any violence has been or will be attempted, and say they can stand the strike better than the operators can. They also claim that the Italians are disgusted and discouraged, and that the experiment, so far as the one is concerned, is a failure. Some of the miners offer to go to work at a reduction if the operators will show that the price of coal is too low to admit of the wages demanded being paid, but this is refused and the lock out will continue.

The Future

Both parties are full of determination. Much bitterness prevails, and miners and operators seem to hate each other with an intensity that is hard to believe. The attack on Fassett, the editor, whom the miners regard as the big gun of their cause, has done much to widen the breach. The citizens are divided in their opinion on the subject.

APPENDIX 7

THE ITALIANS WHO CAME TO COALBURG
IN MARCH 1873

The names in the following tables are drawn from Charles Carr's January 5, 1925 *Youngstown Vindicator* article that cited Marco Antonelli as the source. According to the informant, these are some of the men who arrived as hires during the miners' strike. The four closely placed towns all lie within today's Isernia Province. In 1925, they would have been identified

Carovilli		Agnone	
Vindicator Names	**Suggested Spellings**	**Vindicator Spellings**	**Suggested Spellings**
Luigi Silvestro	*Silvestri*	Felice Menaldi	
Argancelo Di Giacomo	*Arcangelo Di Giacomo*	Piaffacle Serrithio	*Raffaele Serricchio*
Fedele Giacomo	*Di Giacomo*	Filippo Marcovecchio	
Pasquale De Giacomo	*Di Giacomo*	Marco Antonelli	
Gennaro Iannacone	*Iannarone*	Stefano Colucci	
Pasquale Iacobini		John Gentile	
Giovanni Attanasio		Francesco Di Laggaro	*Di Lazzaro*
Achillo	*Achille*	Giuseppe Del Bello	*Di Bello*
Giovanni Cristoforo		Domenico Bartolomeo	
		Raffaele Di Servia	

Pietrabbondante		Roccamandolfi	
Vindicator Names	**Suggested Spellings**	**Vindicator Names**	**Suggested Spellings**
Giovanni Tantangelo	*Santangelo, Tantangelo*	Amadio Cialetti	*Amedeo*
Silvestro Vitullo	*Vitullo, Vitiello*	Sabbatino Cialett	*Sabatino Cialelli*
Domenicantonio Vitullo		Angelo Icasella	
Aliodore Zarlenga	*Aliodoro*	Michele di Marco	also *De Marco*
Angencelo Bartolomeo	*Angelantonio*		
Alfonso Saulino e Moglie	Moglie is "wife" in Italian		
Michele Formichele			
Masto Rocco Sanangelo	*Santangelo*		

The Coalburg Italians and their home towns, as listed by Marco Antonelli in the *Youngstown Vindicator* on January 5, 1925. *Joe Tucciarone.*

as municipalities in the province of Campobasso. Salvatore Papale, whose ancestor lived in Hubbard Township, supplied the suggested spellings. Other records identify Alfonso and Maria Saulino as having emigrated from Agnone. Also, Joseph Butler maintains that Colucci was from Avellino.

THE MURDER OF GIOVANNI CHIESA

This account of Giovanni Chiesa's murder appeared on page two of the *Northern Ohio Journal* on Saturday, August 9, 1873:

From the Youngstown Register we condense the following: On last Sunday afternoon an outbreak took place at Church Hill, which surpasses in the horrible character of its details, anything that we have ever heard of before. The immediate cause of the trouble was a quarrel between a miner named William Trotter and an Italian, John Church. Church, seeing he was overpowered, ran for a house where the rest of the Italians were, and when he got to the door cried to be let in. A short time after he had been admitted into the house a large crowd numbering from fifty to a hundred of the union miners gathered around the house and commenced throwing stones and brick bats through the windows. There were in the house seven Italians and a German. These men kept the door shut until the stones and bricks began to come through the window in such quantity as to make the place untenable. They then went up stairs into the garret of the building. After that an attempt was made by the rioters to overturn the house. At about the same time several broke into the lower room and discovered that the inmates were in the garret. Finding that the Italians were able to keep them from rushing up the steep and narrow stairs they hesitated a while and then went systematically to work to burn the house and the Italians in it. They took the furniture and broke it up, and piled it in the middle of the floor and set fire to it. After the house had been set on fire the rioters withdrew to the outside and held the door, and stood by the windows of the burning house with clubs to drive the Italians back into the fire if they should try to come out! But a ring leader named William Parden interfered and said, "Let them have fair play. Let them out." The first man that came out of the house was the German whose name is Butts. He was allowed to go to one side after having given a promise that he would not go away nor call the constables. After that the Italians followed and as fast as they came out they were knocked down first by the merciful Parden and then kicked and knocked and beaten and stoned by the whole of the rioters. As soon as a poor wretch of an Italian would recover his senses from the beating which he had received from the crowd of rioters he would try to crawl off only to receive a kicking, and beating, and stoning from another crowd. The detail of the miners given in testimony at the inquest was almost incredible. One miner wore his heavy boots all to pieces in kicking the prostrate Italians. When Church came out of the burning house, he was first knocked down by the fists of the rioters, by clubs, by stones, and was kicked and pounded well after he was down. Recovering his senses enough to try to make his escape, he passed by a Scotchman working for the Niles Coal Co., whose name is not yet learned. This man had a gun in his hands, and as Church tried to escape, he struck him over the head with it, so heavily that the stock of the gun was broken off. This blow felled the poor wretch to the ground, but the man continued and struck him two or three more blows with the barrel. These blows, as has been shown by the medical examination, fractured the skull of the Italian. After he fell and lay there, the rioters crowded around him, kicking and beating him. The testimony shows that at one time two men got upon the poor wretch, one upon his body, and the other upon his head, and actually stamped and jumped upon him for some moments. This was close to the burning house, and after a little, the heat became so intense that these fiends went away (probably to join the chase after the other Italians), leaving the dying man there in the scorching heat that they themselves were unable to endure. When the building had burned down, some of them went back, probably out of mere curiosity to see whether Church was alive or not. He had life enough left to moan out a request for water, and the brutal fiends picked him up and dragged him a little way and threw him into a mud puddle with the remark that he could get all the water he wanted there. The poor Italian, who it seemed was a man of extraordinary vitality, mustered up strength enough to crawl out of the puddle, and fell over on his face, dead. We refrain from any further description of such horrible scenes of brutality. John Church was past all help. His comrades managed, after receiving terrible beatings, and fearful injuries, to get beyond the reach of the rioters. One man reached Seceder Corners with both arms broken. Another reached the same place with injuries that are expected to prove fatal. A third is reported missing and is supposed to be lying dead somewhere in the woods. The others escaped in different directions with greater or lesser injuries. Late on Tuesday night the coroner's jury brought in a verdict to the effect that the Italian came to his death by blows given by Wm. Parden, John Watson, John Neal, Alex. Hodge, Hugh Trotter, Wm. Baxter, and others, known and unknown to the jury. The disposition of the miners toward the Italians is shown by the fact that two or three weeks previous the house in which they lived had been stoned so there was not a whole window in it, and none of the Italians had dared to go outside of it for fear of being stoned by the old miners, who, it seems, were always on the alert to persecute them. And yet the Italians were so patient under this treatment that they made no complaint, and Mr. Morris, the manager of the works knew nothing about their persecutions until last Saturday morning.

APPENDIX 9

THE *CLEVELAND DAILY LEADER* CONDEMNS ALONZO FASSETT

The *Cleveland Daily Leader*'s September 4, 1873 attack on Alonzo Fassett and his pro-miner newspaper included these serious charges:

The Miner and Manufacturer, published in Youngstown, and beyond all question the thinnest, weakest and most puerile daily newspaper ever published in America, does the Leader the honor to disagree with its opinion of a good deal that is called "labor reform" in politics. The M. & M. thinks that the Leader is dishonest in its opposition to the workingmen. Without caring to discuss that point at length, we have one opinion upon a similar subject, which we can warrant as honest. It is this: That the editor of the Miner and Manufacturer, who was mainly responsible for precipitating and prolonging the strike of the coal miners in the Mahoning Valley last winter, by which the miners were kept idle for three months, the miners and their families reduced to the verge of starvation, and the whole industry of the Mahoning Valley paralyzed, was guilty of a crime which should make him hide his head with shame and remorse for the rest of his life. The results of that strike were first, riot and murder, for which six men are now in prison to be tried for their lives; secondly, the loss of the control of the Cleveland market by the Mahoning Valley operators and the changing of our source of supply to the Tuscarawas and Hocking coal regions; thirdly, the reduction of the miners to penury and want, bringing them into hostility with their employers, which only made their final defeat more humiliating. All through the long months of the strike the Leader endeavored to persuade the strikers to resume work, while the Miner and Manufacturer—then a weekly—exhorted them to hold out and maintain the fight to the bitter end. We ask the miners and their employers today to say which paper gave the better advice. Whoever speaks the plain truth about the labor question must state some straightforward, unpleasant facts, and when a newspaper or an orator does this it is a higher and better service performed than that of the demagogue who deceives his hearers by telling them that labor rules the world, and by holding up promises and expectations that can never be realized.

APPENDIX 10

FILIPPO CAROSELLA, FILIPPO MARCOVECCHIO, ALFONSO SAULINO AND ANGELA MARIA SAULINO

Five hundred forty-nine Italian immigrants boarded the steamship *Erin* at Le Havre on December 10, 1872. They arrived in the Port of New York on January 1, 1873. Among the Italians were Filippo Carosella, age forty-four, Filippo Marcovecchio, age thirty-three, Alfonso Saulino, age twenty-three, and Angela Saulino, age twenty. The 1880 census for Hubbard, Ohio, included a colony of Italian coal miners. They lived on a parcel of land formerly owned by the Mahoning Coal Railroad Company in the community of Coalburg. Among the Italians listed on the census were Philip Carsela, age fifty-three, Philip Marquet, age forty, Alfonso Saulino, age thirty, and Mary A. Saulino, age forty. Records show Philip Marquet was Filippo Marcovecchio, Philip Carsela was Filippo Carosella and Mary A. Saulino was Angela Maria Saulino. Were these four Italians on the 1880 census the same four people who immigrated on the steamship *Erin*? Old documents are fragmentary and incomplete, but in this case, they provide a wealth of information.

Making this case would be impossible if the four Italians had common surnames like Rossi, Esposito or Ferrari. However, there are relatively few Carosellas, Marcovecchios or Saulinos in Italy. In addition, most of them are from the area in and around the Molise, strengthening the claim that the four Italians on the *Erin* were the four Italians in Coalburg. In fact, documents show the four Coalburg Italians were all from Agnone. For example, the 1929 obituary of Mercede Carosella, the widow of Filippo, stated she was born on April 1, 1855, in the comune of Agnone.[397] A marriage record in Agnone listed the wedding of a Filippo Carosella to a Mercede Agnone in 1872.

The Ancestry.com database is a comprehensive archive that includes information about Italian immigrants to the United States. There are many Filippo (or Philip) Marcovecchios in these records, but the Marcovecchio on the 1880 Coalburg census was the only one born before 1878. Further evidence indicates that Filippo Marcovecchio was in Coalburg in 1873. Records show he and his wife, Merceda, had a daughter, Gabriella, who was born in 1867. In May 1898, during the trial of her son's murderer, Gabriella (Marcovecchio) Ferrando stated she had lived in the United States for twenty-five years.[398] She was only six years old in 1873, so it's likely she was living with her parents at that time. This would argue for Filippo's presence in Coalburg in 1873.

In the related case of Filippo Carosella, only one individual by that name appears in the Ancestry.com archives, and he was in Coalburg at the time of the 1880 census. It is likely Carosella and Marcovecchio were passengers on the *Erin*.

Alfonso Saulino's 1931 death certificate, filed in Mahoning County, listed Youngstown as his residence, his wife as Angela Maria and their birthplace as Agnone, Campobasso. Joseph Sacchini's 1997 study, *The Italians of Youngstown and the Mahoning Valley, Ohio*, names Saulino as one of that city's prominent Italian immigrants. The author asserts that Saulino arrived in New York on New Year's Day 1873 and went directly to Coalburg. This links him to both the steamship *Erin* and the other two Agnonesi.

The Italian immigrants aboard the *Erin* arrived in New York the day the miners' strike of 1873 began. With the Youngstown mines shut down, the ship's passengers would have been in the right place to be recruited by the agent of the Mahoning Coal Company, who arrived at Castle Garden on March 18, 1873. Had they been contracted by him to work in the Coalburg mines, it is likely that some of them would have still been there at the taking of the 1880 census, mining coal or working for one of the railroads. The census of 1880 shows that Alfonso Saulino, Angela Maria Saulino, Filippo Carosella and Filippo Marcovecchio resided in Coalburg. It also shows that Filippo Carosella and Filippo Marcovecchio were employed mining coal.

APPENDIX 11
MAPS

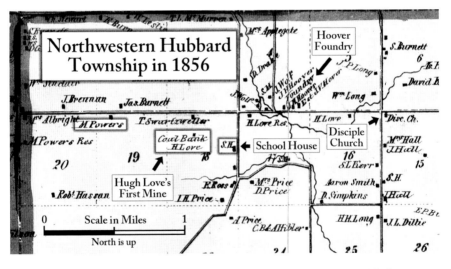

Northwestern Hubbard Township in 1856 included Hugh Love's coal bank, Madison Powers's property and a foundry. *The Library of Congress.*

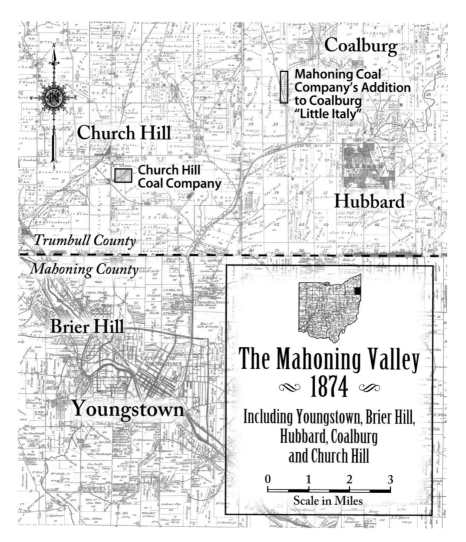

The Mahoning Valley in 1874 included Brier Hill, Coalburg, Hubbard and Church Hill.
The Library of Congress.

Northwestern Hubbard Township in 1874 included Coalburg. *The Library of Congress.*

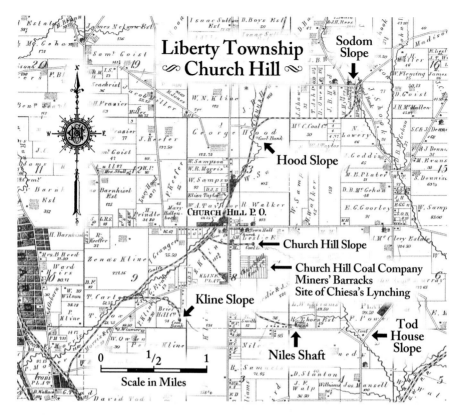

Church Hill is shown in the center of Liberty Township in 1874. *The Library of Congress.*

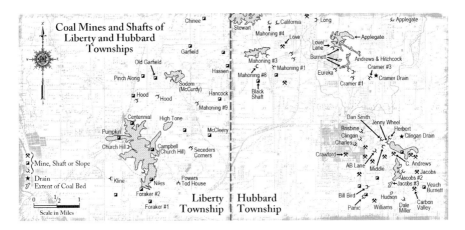

The Liberty and Hubbard coal mines are shown on this map. *The Ohio Department of Natural Resources and the Library of Congress.*

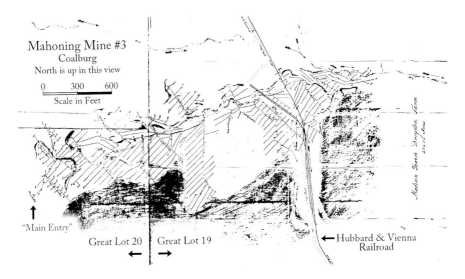

This map of Mahoning Mine Number 3 in Coalburg shows its maze of underground passageways. Names of property owners on adjacent lots (not shown here) date this map to before 1899. Madison Powers originally managed this mine until the operation was assumed by the Mahoning Coal Company. *Ann Harris,* Abandoned Coal Mines, *Youngstown State University.*

NOTES

Preface

1. Cicero, *Brutus, Orator*, trans. G.L. Hendrickson and H.M. Hubbell, Loeb Classical Library 342 (Cambridge, MA: Harvard University Press, 1939), 395, DOI: 10.4159/DLCL.marcus_tullius_cicero-orator.1939.

2. Herbert G. Gutman, "The Buena Vista Affair, 1874–1875," *Pennsylvania Magazine of History and Biography* 88, no. 3 (July 1964): 251, https://journals.psu.edu/pmhb/article/view/41962/41683.

3. Herbert G. Gutman "Reconstruction in Ohio: Negroes in the Hocking Valley Coal Mines in 1873 and 1874," *Labor History* 3, no. 3 (1962): 243, DOI: 10.1080/00236566208583905.

4. Priscilla Long, *Where the Sun Never Shines: A History of America's Bloody Coal Industry* (New York: Paragon House, 1989), 114.

5. *Youngstown, Past and Present* (Cleveland: Wiggins & McKillop, 1875), 53–62, https://hdl.handle.net/2027/loc.ark:/13960/t2q52wp9d.

6. Andrew Roy, *A History of the Coal Miners of the United States from the Development of the Mines to the Close of the Anthracite Strike of 1902* (Columbus, OH: J.L. Trauger, 1907), 136–38, https://www.google.com/books/?id=BJtIAAAAYAAJ.

7. "Modocery! Murder and Arson at Church Hill," *Mahoning Vindicator*, August 1, 1873, 8, https://news.google.com/newspapers?nid=ib87rSy7x5MC&dat=18730808.

8. Edward A. Wieck, *The American Miners' Association, A Record of the Origins of Coal Miners' Unions in the United States* (New York: Russell Sage Foundation, 1940), 141.

Chapter 1

9. Appendix 2 records the few appearances of Coalburg's name in government documents.

10. Alphonso Hart and James Somerville, "A Natural Curiosity," *Portage (OH) Sentinel*, March 5, 1857, 2, https://chroniclingamerica.loc.gov/lccn/sn83035102/1857-03-05/ed-1/seq-2/.

11. H.C., "Trumbull Coal: Visit to the Mines and the Information Mined Therefrom," *Cleveland Leader*, April 7, 1879, 2, https://www.genealogybank.com/newspapers/sourcelist.

12. "Coal Discovery in Liberty," *Warren Western Reserve Chronicle*, June 18, 1862, 3, https://chroniclingamerica.loc.gov/lccn/sn84028385/1862-06-18/ed-1/seq-3/.

13. William Ritezel, "Coal at Church Hill," *Warren Western Reserve Chronicle*, May 15, 1867, 3, https://chroniclingamerica.loc.gov/lccn/sn84028385/1867-05-15/ed-1/seq-3/.

14. William Ritezel, *Warren Western Reserve Chronicle*, December 16, 1868, 3, https://chroniclingamerica.loc.gov/lccn/sn84028385/1868-12-16/ed-1/seq-3/.

15. Ibid.

16. Ritezel, "Coal at Church Hill."

17. "Filed Yesterday," *Daily Ohio Statesman*, June 4, 1868, 3, https://chroniclingamerica.loc.gov/lccn/sn84028645/1868-06-04/ed-1/seq-3/.

18. Ritezel, *Warren Western Reserve Chronicle*, December 16, 1868, 3.

19. Andrew Roy, *Sixth Annual Report of the State Inspector of Mines, to the Governor of the State of Ohio, for the Year 1880* (Columbus, OH: G.J. Brand & Co., 1881), 24, https://www.hathitrust.org/.

20. Clayton J. Ruminski, *Iron Valley: The Transformation of the Iron Industry in Ohio's Mahoning Valley, 1802–1913* (Columbus: Trillium, Ohio State University Press, 2017), 43.

21. "Local Facts and Trivia: Nebo," Public Library of Youngstown and Mahoning County, accessed November 6, 2017, http://www.libraryvisit.org/research/local-resources/local-facts-and-trivia/.

22. "The Great Iron and Coal Region of Ohio," *Cleveland Daily Plain Dealer*, March 31, 1851, 2, https://www.genealogybank.com/newspapers/sourcelist.

23. "King Coal," *Cleveland Daily Plain Dealer*, January 31, 1873, 3, https://www.genealogybank.com/newspapers/sourcelist.

24. Andrew Roy, *Eighth Annual Report of the State Inspector of Mines, to the Governor of the State of Ohio, for the Year 1882* (Columbus, OH: G.J. Brand & Co., 1882), 12, https://www.google.com/books?id=_ngAAAAMAAJ.

25. Kenneth Cottingham, "The Influence of Geology in Ohio Place Names," *Ohio Journal of Science* 49, no. 1 (1949): 36, https://kb.osu.edu/dspace/bitstream/handle/1811/3678/V49N01_034.pdf.

26. Mark S. Tochtenhagen, "Mine Subsidence and the History of Coal Mining in the Mahoning Valley" (senior thesis, Ohio State University, 1985), 7, https://pdfsecret.com/download/mine-subsidence-and-the-history-of-coal-mining-in-the-mahoning-valley-a-senior-_5a132c96d64ab24772a76508_pdf.

27. "Ohio Legislature," *Daily Ohio Statesman*, January 28, 1846, 2, https://www.genealogybank.com/newspapers/sourcelist.

28. "Home Industries: The Mahoning Iron Works," *Cleveland Daily Leader*, April 11, 1868, 4, https://www.genealogybank.com/newspapers/sourcelist.

29. James Moore Swank, *History of the Manufacture of Iron in All Ages: And Particularly in the United States for Three Hundred Years, from 1585 to 1885* (Philadelphia: published by the author, 1884), 239, https://books.google.com/books?id=EQsKAAAAIAAJ.

30. "Varieties," *New York Herald*, August 26, 1846, 2, https://chroniclingamerica.loc.gov/lccn/sn83030313/1846-08-26/ed-1/seq-2/.

31. "Early Iron Enterprises in the Far West," in *1880 Census, vol. 2: Report on the Manufactures of the United States* (Washington: U.S. Census Bureau, 1880), 119, https://www2.census.gov/library/publications/decennial/1880/vol-02-manufactures/1880_v2-17.pdf.

Chapter 2

32. See Appendix 3 for a list of Church Hill and Coalburg mines.

33. "Hubbard Branch Railroad," *Mahoning Register*, reprinted in the *Warren Western Reserve Chronicle*, November 5, 1862, 3, https://chroniclingamerica.loc.gov/lccn/sn84028385/1862-11-05/ed-1/seq-3/.

34. "Fossil Forests: Visit to the Great Coal Region of the Mahoning Valley," *Chicago Republican*, April 6, 1868, 5, https://www.genealogybank.com/newspapers/sourcelist.

35. "Gored to Death: Wealthy Old Farmer of Mahoning County Killed by Bull—Strange Whim," *Canton Repository*, April 13, 1899, 6, https://www.genealogybank.com/newspapers/sourcelist.

36. Harriet Taylor Upton, *A Twentieth Century History of Trumbull County, Ohio* (Chicago: Lewis Publishing Company, 1909), 2:397, https://books.google.com/books?id=-xoVAAAAYAAJ.

37. *Atlas and Directory of Trumbull County, Ohio: Including a Directory of Freeholders and Official Register of the County* (Cleveland: American Atlas Company, 1899; Evansville, IN: Unigraphic, 1979), 177, https://hdl.handle. net/2027/uiug.30112024781699.

38. Upton, *Twentieth Century History*, 2:399.

39. Ibid., 2:398.

40. Ibid.

41. Ibid.

42. Joseph Green Butler, *History of Youngstown and the Mahoning Valley, Ohio* (Chicago: American Historical Society, 1921), 2:169, https://books. google.com/books?id=iRgVAAAAYAAJ.

43. Family Search, "Ohio, Trumbull County Records, 1795–2010," accessed October 5, 2018, https://www.familysearch. org/ark:/61903/3:1:3QS7-L9Q6-FWRK?i=466&wc=Q64Q-WP4%3A1055417201%2C1589207917&cc=2065327.

44. Henry Howe, *Historical Collections of Ohio in Two Volumes* (Cincinnati: C.J. Krehbiel & Co., 1888), 1:113.

45. Ibid., 1:114.

46. Douglas L. Crowell, *Investigation and Inventory of Abandoned Underground Mines in Columbiana, Mahoning, and Trumbull Counties, Ohio* (Columbus, OH: Department of Natural Resources, 1980), 29, https://geosurvey. ohiodnr.gov/portals/geosurvey/PDFs/OpenFileReports/OFR_1980-1_DataSheets_TrumbullCo.pdf.

47. "Coal: The Trade in Anthracite and Bituminous," *Chicago Tribune*, April 15, 1868, 5, https://www.genealogybank.com/newspapers/sourcelist.

48. "His Life Ended," *Cleveland Daily Plain Dealer*, December 26, 1893, 2, https://www.genealogybank.com/newspapers/sourcelist.

49. In 1895, New Lisbon was renamed Lisbon.

50. "He Is Gone," *Youngstown Weekly Telegram*, December 28, 1893, 2.

51. Ibid.

52. Ibid., 4.

53. "Speech of Hon. David Tod," *Cleveland Morning Leader*, October 2, 1861, 2, https://chroniclingamerica.loc.gov/lccn/sn83035143/1861-10-02/ed-1/seq-2/.

Chapter 3

54. Butler, *History of Youngstown*, 1:199, https://books.google.com/books?id=IRgVAAAAYAAJ.

55. *Cleveland Daily Leader*, September 8, 1870, 2, https://www.genealogybank.com/newspapers/sourcelist.

56. Whitelaw Reid, *Ohio in the War: Her Statesmen, Generals and Soldiers, Volume II: The History of Her Regiments and Other Military Organizations* (Cincinnati: Robert Clarke Company, 1895), 492, https://books.google.com/books?id=WCRXAAAAYAAJ.

57. Ruminski, *Iron Valley*, 104 (see n. 20).

58. Ibid.

59. Ibid.

60. "Family Reading: The Mahoning Valley," *Weekly Ohio Farmer*, December 2, 1865, 6, https://www.genealogybank.com/newspapers/sourcelist.

61. Ibid.

62. "Cleveland, Brown & Co's Iron and Nails Warehouse," *Cleveland Morning Leader*, February 3, 1865, 4, https://www.genealogybank.com/newspapers/sourcelist.

63. Charles Carr, "Brown-Bonnell's," *Youngstown Sunday Vindicator*, February 13, 1910, 23, https://news.google.com/newspapers?id=viJIAAAAIBAJ&sjid=F4EMAAAAIBAJ&pg=4285%2C4763800.

64. "Mahoning Valley, Youngstown, Its Rolling Mills, Blast Furnaces and Coal Mines," *Pittsburgh Iron World and Manufacturer*, March 12, 1872, 1, https://www.genealogybank.com/newspapers/sourcelist.

Chapter 4

65. Matteo Pretelli, *L'emigrazione italiana negli Stati Uniti* (Bologna: Società editrice il Mulino, 2011), 38.

66. Ibid., 36.

67. Italian emigration historian Francesco P. Cerase references P. Sylos Labini's quote from *Problemi dello sviluppo económico*: "La occupazione è altamente precaria nelle zone agrarie in cui prevalgono le colture cerealicole." *Un secolo di emigrazione italiana: 1876–1976*, ed. Gianfausto Rosoli (Rome: Centro Studi Emigrazione, 1978), 117.

68. Christopher Duggan, *A Concise History of Italy* (New York: Cambridge University Press, 1994), 118.

69. Denis Mack Smith, *Modern Italy: A Political History* (Ann Arbor: University of Michigan Press, 1997), 71.

70. Luigi Campanelli, *Il Territorio di Capracotta: Note, memorie, spigolature* (Ferentino: Scuola Tip. Antoniana, 1931), 154.

71. U.S. Bureau of the Census, "Migration," chap. C in *Historical Statistics of the United States: Colonial Times to 1957, A Statistical Abstract Supplement* (Washington, D.C.: Government Printing Office, 1960), 57, https://www2.census.gov/library/publications/1960/compendia/hist_stats_colonial-1957/hist_stats_colonial-1957-chC.pdf.

72. "The Italian Emigrants," *New York Herald*, December 12, 1872, 10, https://www.genealogybank.com/newspapers/sourcelist.

73. Family Search, "New York Passenger Lists, 1820–1891," accessed October 5, 2018, https://www.familysearch.org/search/image/index?owc=https://www.familysearch.org/service/cds/recapi/sord/collection/1849782/waypoints.

74. Appendix 4 describes the tremendous rise in emigration from Italy that occurred in the autumn of 1872.

75. William A. Douglass, *Emigration in a South Italian Town: An Anthropological History* (New Brunswick, NJ: Rutgers University Press, 1984), 74.

76. Ibid., 5.

77. *Agnonesi* refers to residents of Agnone.

78. Douglass, *Emigration in a South Italian Town*, 65.

79. Ibid., 63.

80. Charlotte Erickson, *American Industry and the European Immigrant: 1860–1885* (Cambridge, MA: Harvard University Press, 1957), 84.

81. "The Pauper Italians," *New York Herald*, November 23, 1872, 11, https://chroniclingamerica.loc.gov/lccn/sn83030313/1872-11-23/ed-1/seq-11/.

82. "The Italians: More of the Emigration Machinery—Work Wanted for Willing Men," *New York Herald*, January 4, 1873, 8, https://chroniclingamerica.loc.gov/lccn/sn83030313/1873-01-04/ed-1/seq-8/.

83. Ibid.

84. "Avviso agli emigranti in America," *Gazzetta della Provincia di Molise*, December 26, 1872, 3, http://bibliotecadigitale.provincia.campobasso.it:81/easynet/WaterMarkGenerator.asp?Code=PeriodiciMolisani&VFilePath=Archivi/PeriodiciMolisani/All/0003/3281A.JPG&Quality=75.

85. No evidence exists that bogus agents persuaded the four Agnonesi to emigrate, but it's highly likely it occurred, since other Italians aboard the *Erin*, who were from the same region, testified they were induced by fraudulent advertisements to book passage to the United States.

86. "Emigrants' Wrongs," *New York Tribune*, November 22, 1872, 1, https://chroniclingamerica.loc.gov/lccn/sn83030214/1872-11-22/ed-1/seq-1/.

87. Nicholas J. Evans, "Work in Progress: Indirect Passage from Europe Transmigration Via the UK, 1836–1914," *Journal for Maritime Research* 3 no. 1 (June 2001): 70, http://www.tandfonline.com/doi/abs/10.1080/21533369.2001.9668313.

88. "The Immigrant Italians: What Caused Them to Leave Sunny Italy for America," *New York Herald*, January 3, 1873, 10, https://chroniclingamerica.loc.gov/lccn/sn83030313/1873-01-03/ed-1/seq-10/.

89. Another emigrant from Agnone, Antonio Mastronardi, boarded the *Erin*, but he parted company with the other four Agnonesi when the ship reached New York. He would settle in Vicksburg, Mississippi.

90. Joseph P. McDonnell, "The Ocean Steerage Abuses," *New York Herald*, January 27, 1873, 11, https://chroniclingamerica.loc.gov/lccn/sn83030313/1873-01-27/ed-1/seq-11/.

91. Ibid.

92. "Starvation at Sea," *New York Sun*, January 2, 1873, 2, https://chroniclingamerica.loc.gov/lccn/sn83030272/1873-01-02/ed-1/seq-2/.

93. "The Immigrant Italians," *New York Herald*, January 3, 1873, 10.

94. *New York Sun*, January 28, 1873, 2, https://chroniclingamerica.loc.gov/lccn/sn83030272/1873-01-28/ed-1/seq-2/.

95. "The Farmer's Opportunity," *New York Sun*, May 1, 1873, 2, https://chroniclingamerica.loc.gov/lccn/sn83030272/1873-05-01/ed-1/seq-2/.

96. "The New York *Commercial Advertiser* Contains the Following Editorial," *New Orleans Republican*, January 15, 1873, 8, https://chroniclingamerica.loc.gov/lccn/sn83016555/1873-01-15/ed-1/seq-8/.

97. "City Intelligence: Labor Exchange at Castle Garden," *New York Evening Post*, November 4, 1867, 4, https://www.genealogybank.com/newspapers/sourcelist.

Chapter 5

98. Rev. John McDowell, "The Life of a Coal Miner," *Coal Mining in the Gilded Age and Progressive Era*, Ohio State University, Department of History, last accessed October 4, 2018, https://ehistory.osu.edu/exhibitions/gildedage/content/LifeofaCoalMiner.

99. George Elmer Fiedler, *A Historical Story of East Hubbard (Township) and Parts of Hubbard and Pennsylvania* (Hubbard, OH: Fiedler, 1976), 90.

100. McDowell, "The Life of a Coal Miner."

101. Carter Goodrich, *The Miner's Freedom: A Study of the Working Life in a Changing Industry* (Boston: Marshall Jones Company, 1925), 15.

102. Ibid., 20.

103. *Cincinnati Daily Gazette*, November 15, 1879, 4, https://www.genealogybank.com/newspapers/sourcelist.

104. "Local and Personal," *Warren Western Reserve Chronicle*, August 10, 1870, 3, https://chroniclingamerica.loc.gov/lccn/sn84028385/1870-08-10/ed-1/seq-3/. John Matthews, mine boss during the crisis at the Powers bank, was killed by a faulty explosive in the very same pit on August 3, 1870.

105. Andrew Roy, *Third Annual Report of the State Mine Inspector, to the Governor of the State of Ohio, for the Year 1876, Executive Documents: Part 2* (Columbus, OH: Nevins & Myers, State Printers, 1876), 67.

106. Andrew Roy, "The Perils of the Mine: Leaves from the Note Book of a Mine Inspector," *Coal Trade Journal* 23 (January 2–December 31, 1884), 717, https://hdl.handle.net/2027/pst.000060210210.

107. Ibid.

108. Andrew Roy, *History of the Coal Miners*, 110 (see n. 6).

109. Charles Carr, "Caught in a Mine," *Youngstown Sunday Vindicator*, May 1, 1910, 21, https://news.google.com/newspapers?id=yCJIAAAAIBAJ&sjid=F4EMAAAAIBAJ&pg=1059%2C6484163.

110. "Buried Alive," *New York World*, August 9, 1865, 2, https://www.genealogybank.com/newspapers/sourcelist.

111. "Effect of Discovery of Coal Was Influential," *Hubbard News*, September 13, 1934, 15. Alfred Redmond was the first rescuer to reach the Millers; six years later, Redmond was killed when a coal car he was riding broke loose and plummeted to the bottom of a shaft a few miles north of Coalburg.

112. "The Hubbard Coal Bank Accident; Details of the Rescue of the Imprisoned Miners," *Cleveland Leader*, August 5, 1865, 1, https://www.genealogybank.com/newspapers/sourcelist.

113. Ibid.

114. For detailed descriptions of two Hubbard Township mines, see Appendix 5.

115. In that tragedy, 110 workers were suffocated when a massive fire blocked the only exit of Avondale's Steuben Shaft in Luzerne County, Pennsylvania.

116. Quentin R. Skrabec, *William McKinley, Apostle of Protectionism* (New York: Algora Publishing, 2008), 65, https://books.google.com/books?isbn=0875865771.

117. John Benson and Robert G. Neville, *Studies in the Yorkshire Coal Industry* (Fairfield, NJ: Augustus M. Kelley, 1976), ix.

118. Ronald L. Lewis, *Welsh Americans: A History of Assimilation in the Coalfields* (Chapel Hill: University of North Carolina Press, 2008), 176, https://books.google.com/books?isbn=0807887900.

119. "Miner's Meeting at Church Hill," *Warren Western Reserve Chronicle*, September 28, 1870, 3, https://chroniclingamerica.loc.gov/lccn/sn84028385/1870-09-28/ed-1/seq-3/.

120. "Miners' Convention," *Warren Western Reserve Chronicle*, November 16, 1870, 2, https://chroniclingamerica.loc.gov/lccn/sn84028385/1870-11-16/ed-1/seq-2/.

121. "Meeting of Coal Miners at Youngstown," *Cincinnati Daily Gazette*, March 21, 1871, 1, https://www.genealogybank.com/newspapers/sourcelist.

122. "Miners' Convention," *Mahoning Vindicator*, March 21, 1871, 3, https://news.google.com/newspapers?nid=ib87rSy7x5MC&dat=18710321.

123. "The New Mining Bill," *Mahoning Vindicator*, April 24, 1874, 7, https://news.google.com/newspapers?nid=ib87rSy7x5MC&dat=18740417.

Chapter 6

124. William Ritezel, *Warren Western Reserve Chronicle*, January 29, 1868, 3, https://chroniclingamerica.loc.gov/lccn/sn84028385/1868-01-29/ed-1/seq-3/.

125. Edward Orton, "The Coal Seams of the Lower Measures of Ohio," in *Report of the Geological Survey of Ohio, vol. 5: Economic Geology* (Columbus, OH: G.J. Brand & Co., 1884), 169.

126. William Ritezel, *Warren Western Reserve Chronicle*, December 4, 1867, 3, https://chroniclingamerica.loc.gov/lccn/sn84028385/1867-12-04/ed-1/seq-3/.

127. William Ritezel, *Warren Western Reserve Chronicle*, December 15, 1869, 3, https://chroniclingamerica.loc.gov/lccn/sn84028385/1869-12-15/ed-1/seq-3/.

128. "Vienna," *Cleveland Daily Leader*, November 23, 1872, 2, https://www.genealogybank.com/newspapers/sourcelist.

129. *Mahoning Vindicator*, November 8, 1872, 5, https://news.google.com/newspapers?nid=ib87rSy7x5MC&dat=18721108.

130. "The Coal Miners Strike and Its Remedy," *Cleveland Daily Leader*, February 13, 1873, 2, https://www.genealogybank.com/newspapers/sourcelist.

131. "Northern Ohio Items," *Cleveland Daily Leader*, December 28, 1872, 4, https://www.genealogybank.com/newspapers/sourcelist.
132. "The Price of Coal Raised," *Cleveland Daily Plain Dealer*, November 6, 1872, 3, https://www.genealogybank.com/newspapers/sourcelist.
133. Eli Perkins, "Strikes among the Ohio Coal Miners," *Cincinnati Commercial*, reprinted in *Warren Western Reserve Chronicle*, February 5, 1873, 3, https://chroniclingamerica.loc.gov/lccn/sn84028385/1873-02-05/ed-1/seq-3/.
134. "King Coal," *Cleveland Daily Plain Dealer*, January 31, 1873, 3, https://www.genealogybank.com/newspapers/sourcelist.
135. "Strike but Hear," *Canton Repository*, February 7, 1873, 2, https://www.genealogybank.com/newspapers/sourcelist.
136. Perkins, "Strikes among the Ohio Coal Miners."

Chapter 7

137. Wieck, *American Miners' Association*, 110 (see n. 8).
138. "Locals from the Niles Independent," *Warren Western Reserve Chronicle*, August 17, 1870, 3, https://chroniclingamerica.loc.gov/lccn/sn84028385/1870-08-17/ed-1/seq-3/.
139. *Hillsborough Highland Weekly News*, July 14, 1870, 3, https://chroniclingamerica.loc.gov/lccn/sn85038158/1870-07-14/ed-1/seq-3/.
140. *Cleveland Daily Plain Dealer*, July 30, 1870, 3, https://www.genealogybank.com/newspapers/sourcelist.
141. "Ohio: Miners' Strike Ended," *Memphis Public Ledger*, August 20, 1870, 3, https://www.genealogybank.com/newspapers/sourcelist.
142. "Disturbance at the Vienna Coal Shaft," *Warren Western Reserve Chronicle*, April 19, 1871, 3, https://chroniclingamerica.loc.gov/lccn/sn84028385/1871-04-19/ed-1/seq-3/.
143. "Here Me Comes," *Ohio Patriot*, January 10, 1873, 3, http://lepper.advantage-preservation.com/Viewer/?t=31261&i=t&by=1873&bdd=1870&d=01011873-12311873&m=between&fn=ohio_patriot_usa_ohio_new_lisbon_18730110_english_3&df=1&dt=10.
144. "Local News," *Canton Repository*, January 31, 1873, 3, https://www.genealogybank.com/newspapers/sourcelist.
145. "Colored Labor as a Remedy for Strikes," *Chicago Post*, January 31, 1873, 1, https://www.genealogybank.com/newspapers/sourcelist.
146. "Here Me Comes," *Ohio Patriot*. *Ohio Patriot* aligned itself with the Democratic Party and its anti-black, anti-Reconstructionist politics.

147. *Nashville Union and American*, February 6, 1873, 2, https://chroniclingamerica.loc.gov/lccn/sn85033699/1873-02-06/ed-1/seq-2/.

148. "Negro Miners," *Mahoning Vindicator*, February 14, 1873, 5, https://news.google.com/newspapers?nid=ib87rSy7x5MC&dat=18730207.

149. John B. Lewis, "The Miner's Strike in the Mahoning Valley," *Cleveland Daily Plain Dealer*, February 11, 1873, 2, https://www.genealogybank.com/newspapers/sourcelist. In the newspaper account, no white hires arrived with the blacks.

150. William Ritezel, "Strikes," *Warren Western Reserve Chronicle*, February 5, 1873, 2, https://chroniclingamerica.loc.gov/lccn/sn84028385/1873-02-05/ed-1/seq-2/.

151. "The Labor Question and Strikes," *Mahoning Vindicator*, February 14, 1873, 1, https://news.google.com/newspapers?nid=ib87rSy7x5MC&dat=18730207.

152. *Warren Western Reserve Chronicle*, February 26, 1873, 3, https://chroniclingamerica.loc.gov/lccn/sn84028385/1873-02-26/ed-1/seq-3/.

153. "The War of Races," *Chicago Daily Tribune*, February 16, 1873, 2, https://chroniclingamerica.loc.gov/lccn/sn84031492/1873-02-16/ed-1/seq-2/.

154. Ibid.

155. Ibid.

156. "The National Labor Congress," *Ottawa (IL) Free Trader*, August 28, 1869, 4, https://chroniclingamerica.loc.gov/lccn/sn84038582/1869-08-28/ed-1/seq-4/.

157. *Middletown (CT) Constitution*, February 26, 1873, 2, https://www.genealogybank.com/newspapers/sourcelist.

158. "Kentucky: The Ivey Murder—The Ku-Klux Troubles in Estell County," *Chicago Tribune*, July 23, 1871, 1, https://chroniclingamerica.loc.gov/lccn/sn82014064/1871-07-23/ed-1/seq-1/.

159. *Daily Illinois State Register*, December 31, 1872, 1, https://www.genealogybank.com/newspapers/sourcelist.

160. Ronald L. Lewis, *Black Coal Miners in America: Race, Class and Community Conflict, 1780–1980* (Lexington: University Press of Kentucky, 2015), 79, https://books.google.com/books?isbn=0813150442.

161. A review of Justis's want ads reveals that he provided employment to whites and immigrant workers as well as African Americans. Job placement opportunities were identified by race, immigrant status or gender.

162. Justis's 1860 census entry includes a schedule showing he owned five slaves on his farm. Although his business office came to be located in the

old slave market, there is no evidence that Justis was a former trader in slaves.

163. *Richmond Daily Dispatch*, March 17, 1868, March 10, 1873, September 4, 1873, May 27, 1875, et al., https://chroniclingamerica.loc.gov/lccn/sn84024738/.

164. Erickson, *American Industry and the European Immigrant*, 111 (see n. 80).

165. Sherman's order was signed on January 16, 1865.

166. Edward Magdol, *A Right to the Land: Essays on the Freedmen's Community*, Contributions in American History Series 61 (Westport, CT: Greenwood Press, 1977), 156.

167. "The Story of Virginia's Reconstruction," accessed May 9, 2019, https://reconstructingvirginia.richmond.edu/overview.

168. William Gillette, *Retreat from Reconstruction 1869–1879* (Baton Rouge: Louisiana State University Press, 1979), 65; "K.K.K.," *Reconstructing Virginia*, https://reconstructingvirginia.richmond.edu/items/show/970.

169. Lewis, *Black Coal Miners in America*, 5–6.

170. "Terrible Explosion: Thirty-Seven Persons Killed," *Washington Sentinel*, March 23, 1855, 2, https://www.genealogybank.com/newspapers/sourcelist. On March 19, 1855, an explosion in the Midlothian Coal Pits near Richmond, Virginia, took the lives of thirty-six miners, twenty-nine of whom were black.

171. *Richmond Daily Dispatch*, September 30, 1870, 1, https://chroniclingamerica.loc.gov/lccn/sn84024738/1870-09-30/ed-1/seq-1/.

172. *Richmond Daily Dispatch*, June 21, 1872, 4, https://chroniclingamerica.loc.gov/lccn/sn84024738/1872-06-21/ed-1/seq-4/.

173. William Cohen, *At Freedom's Edge: Black Mobility and the Southern White Quest for Racial Control, 1861–1915* (Baton Rouge: Louisiana State University Press, 1991), 118. In Justis's ad in the December 13, 1872, *Richmond Daily Dispatch*, he promises "high wages," "houses" and fuel as part of the contract to work the New Lisbon mines. Records confirm the practice, at least by one employment agency dealing in black workers, of advertising paid transportation to the destination including rations and lodgings with a parcel of land to farm.

174. Ritezel, "Strikes" (see n. 150).

175. "Colored Laborers Going West," *Alexandria Daily State Journal*, March 18, 1873, 1, https://chroniclingamerica.loc.gov/lccn/sn84024670/1873-03-18/ed-1/seq-1/.

176. "The Brazil Broils: Strategy of the Strikers," *Indianapolis Sentinel*, March 27, 1873, 5, https://www.genealogybank.com/newspapers/sourcelist.

177. "The Trouble in Indiana," *Cleveland Daily Leader*, April 19, 1873, 2, https://www.genealogybank.com/newspapers/sourcelist.

178. "Riot at Knightsville, Ind.," *Wheeling (WV) Intelligencer*, April 16, 1873, 1, https://chroniclingamerica.loc.gov/lccn/sn84026844/1873-04-16/ed-1/seq-1/.

179. "The Trouble in Indiana," *Cleveland Daily Leader*.

180. "Two Thousand Coal Miners on a Strike," *Cincinnati Daily Enquirer*, April 2, 1874, 1, https://www.genealogybank.com/newspapers/sourcelist.

181. "Columbus; The Hocking Valley Coal Miners' Strike," *Cincinnati Commercial*, April 10, 1874, 5, https://www.genealogybank.com/newspapers/sourcelist.

182. "The Striking Miners," *Indianapolis Sentinel*, June 12, 1874, 1, https://www.genealogybank.com/newspapers/sourcelist.

183. "Hocking Valley Miners: An Exciting Day at the Nelsonville Mines," *Chicago Daily Tribune*, June 13, 1874, 7, https://chroniclingamerica.loc.gov/lccn/sn84031492/1874-06-13/ed-1/seq-7/.

184. "Nelsonville Miners' Strike: Five Hundred Colored Men to Take the Place of the Strikers," *Somerset (OH) Press*, June 12, 1874, 2, https://chroniclingamerica.loc.gov/lccn/sn85038088/1874-06-12/ed-1/seq-2/.

185. "The Ohio Miners: The Arrival of the Negro Substitutes at the Mines," *New York Herald*, June 16, 1874, 3, https://chroniclingamerica.loc.gov/lccn/sn83030313/1874-06-16/ed-1/seq-3/.

186. Ibid.

187. "From the Mines," *Indianapolis Sentinel*, June 13, 1874, 1, https://www.genealogybank.com/newspapers/sourcelist.

188. "The Striking Miners," *Indianapolis Sentinel*.

189. "Telegraphic," *Omaha Daily Bee*, June 13, 1874, 1, https://chroniclingamerica.loc.gov/lccn/sn99021999/1874-06-13/ed-1/seq-1/.

190. "The Ohio Miners," *New York Herald*, June 26, 1874, 7, https://www.genealogybank.com/newspapers/sourcelist.

191. Old Miner, "To the Miner's Union," *Jackson (OH) Standard*, July 23, 1874, 3, https://www.genealogybank.com/newspapers/sourcelist.

192. "Some Excitement," *Akron Times*, reprinted in *Stark County (OH) Democrat*, September 14, 1870, 4, https://www.genealogybank.com/newspapers/sourcelist.

193. Ibid.

194. For a full account of Sanford's dealings with the Italian immigrants and their arrival in Coalburg, see Appendix 6.

195. "A Pittsburgher's Opinion of the Strike," *Canton Repository and Republican*, April 25, 1873, 1, https://www.genealogybank.com/newspapers/sourcelist.

196. Charles Carr, "Tales of the City's Industries," *Youngstown Sunday Vindicator*, July 10, 1910, 23, https://news.google.com/newspapers?nid=kFzFP8IdBVAC&dat=19100710&printsec=frontpage&hl=en.

197. "A Pittsburgher's Opinion of the Strike," *Canton Repository and Republican*.

198. "The Strike," *Mahoning Vindicator*, March 28, 1873, 8, https://news.google.com/newspapers?nid=ib87rSy7x5MC&dat=18730321.

199. Ibid.

200. "A Pittsburgher's Opinion of the Strike," *Canton Repository and Republican*.

201. "The Strike," *Mahoning Vindicator*.

202. Andrew Roy, "Church Hill: The Coal Strike—Ejecting the Strikers from the Company's Houses," *Cleveland Leader*, March 18, 1873, 2, https://www.genealogybank.com/newspapers/sourcelist.

203. "Miners' Difficulties," *Memphis Public Ledger*, April 2, 1873, 2, https://chroniclingamerica.loc.gov/lccn/sn85033673/1873-04-02/ed-1/seq-2/.

204. *Mahoning Vindicator*, April 25, 1873, 5, https://news.google.com/newspapers?nid=ib87rSy7x5MC&dat=18730425.

205. "Outrage by Coal Miners on Strike," *New York Herald*, April 30, 1873, 12, https://chroniclingamerica.loc.gov/lccn/sn83030313/1873-04-30/ed-1/seq-12/.

206. William Ritezel, *Warren Western Reserve Chronicle*, May 14, 1873, 3, https://chroniclingamerica.loc.gov/lccn/sn84028385/1873-05-14/ed-1/seq-3/.

Chapter 8

207. *Mahoning Vindicator*, May 9, 1873, 5, https://news.google.com/newspapers?nid=ib87rSy7x5MC&dat=18730509.

208. William Ritezel, *Warren Western Reserve Chronicle*, May 21, 1873, 3, https://chroniclingamerica.loc.gov/lccn/sn84028385/1873-05-21/ed-1/seq-3/.

209. "Ohio News," *Cleveland Daily Plain Dealer*, May 15, 1873, 2, https://www.genealogybank.com/newspapers/sourcelist.

210. *Mahoning Vindicator*, May 16, 1873, 5, https://news.google.com/newspapers?nid=ib87rSy7x5MC&dat=18730516.

211. "Ohio: On a Strike," *Wheeling (WV) Daily Register*, January 31, 1873, 1, https://chroniclingamerica.loc.gov/lccn/sn84026847/1873-01-31/ed-1/seq-1/.

212. William Ritezel, *Warren Western Reserve Chronicle*, April 30, 1873, 2, https://chroniclingamerica.loc.gov/lccn/sn84028385/1873-04-30/ed-1/seq-2/.

213. "Mahoning County—From the *Register* of Youngstown," *Northern Ohio Journal*, May 31, 1873, 2, https://chroniclingamerica.loc.gov/lccn/sn84028194/1873-05-31/ed-1/seq-2/.

214. "The Mahoning Valley Strikers Superseded," *Cleveland Daily Leader*, May 15, 1873, 2, https://www.genealogybank.com/newspapers/sourcelist.

215. George E. McNeill, *The Labor Movement: The Problem of To-Day* (Boston: A.M. Bridgman & Co., 1887), 259.

216. "The Church Hill Coal Company and the Miners' Strike," *Cleveland Daily Leader*, March 19, 1873, 2, https://www.genealogybank.com/newspapers/sourcelist.

217. *Cleveland Leader*, February 8, 1875, 4, https://www.genealogybank.com/newspapers/sourcelist.

218. "Modocery! Murder and Arson at Church Hill," *Mahoning Vindicator* (see n. 7).

219. Ibid.

220. See Appendix 8 for a detailed account of the Church Hill riot and the murder of Giovanni Chiesa.

221. "Modocery! Murder and Arson at Church Hill," *Mahoning Vindicator*.

222. Patrizia Salvetti, *Rope and Soap* (New York: Bordighera Press, 2017), 41. Salvetti claims the first lynching of an Italian in the United States occurred in Vicksburg, Mississippi, on March 25, 1886.

223. "Modocery! Murder and Arson at Church Hill," *Mahoning Vindicator*. "On being arrested and brought before the Justice, in the room where the corpse was lying, these men are said to have exhibited the utmost indifference, and swaggered about as if nothing more than a disputed cock-fight was to be decided."

224. *Mahoning Vindicator*, April 3, 1874, 5, https://news.google.com/newspapers?nid=ib87rSy7x5MC&dat=18740306.

225. *Mahoning Vindicator*, April 10, 1874, 5, https://news.google.com/newspapers?nid=ib87rSy7x5MC&dat=18740410.

226. Butler, *History of Youngstown*, 1:527 (see n. 42).

227. Roy, *History of the Coal Miners*, 69 (see n. 6).

228. Ibid.

229. A few editions of the *Miner and Manufacturer* exist on microform at the Youngstown Public Library.

230. Perkins, "Strikes among the Ohio Coal Miners" (see n. 133).

231. "The Miners' Conspiracy Trial," *New York Herald*, October 4, 1875, 7, https://chroniclingamerica.loc.gov/lccn/sn83030313/1875-10-04/ed-1/seq-7/.

232. "The War Path," *Mahoning Vindicator*, July 25, 1873, 8, https://news.google.com/newspapers?id=37NjAAAAIBAJ&sjid=Z4EMAAAAIBAJ&pg=976%2C6780334.

233. *Puck*, a weekly U.S. periodical, for one.

234. Matthew Frye Jacobson, *Whiteness of a Different Color: European Immigrants and the Alchemy of Race* (Cambridge, MA: Harvard University Press, 1998), 57.

235. Ibid.

236. *Warren Western Reserve Chronicle*, November 16, 1870, 2, https://chroniclingamerica.loc.gov/lccn/sn84028385/1870-11-16/ed-1/seq-2/.

237. *Warren Western Reserve Chronicle*, December 6, 1871, 3, https://chroniclingamerica.loc.gov/lccn/sn84028385/1871-12-06/ed-1/seq-3/.

238. Butler, *History of Youngstown*, 1:350 (see n. 42).

239. "Congressional Convention! Richard Brown, of Mahoning, Nominated for Congress," *Mahoning Vindicator*, August 9, 1872, 1, https://news.google.com/newspapers?id=srNjAAAAIBAJ&sjid=Z4EMAAAAIBAJ&pg=2165%2C4596362.

240. The tin bucket represented the dinner pail carried to work by the common man. "This Brigade is composed exclusively of laboring men—fine haired and kid-gloved gentry being excluded," from "Tin Bucket Brigade," *Mahoning Vindicator*, August 30, 1872, 8, https://news.google.com/newspapers?id=trNjAAAAIBAJ&sjid=Z4EMAAAAIBAJ&pg=1430%2C4762527.

241. *Mahoning Vindicator*, October 4, 1872, 4, https://news.google.com/newspapers?nid=ib87rSy7x5MC&dat=18721004.

242. *Mahoning Vindicator*, September 27, 1872, 1, https://news.google.com/newspapers?nid=ib87rSy7x5MC&dat=18720927.

243. *Mahoning Vindicator*, June 20, 1873, 5, https://news.google.com/newspapers?nid=ib87rSy7x5MC&dat=18730620.

244. "King Coal," *Cleveland Daily Plain Dealer* (see n. 134).

245. See Appendix 9 for the full text of the *Cleveland Daily Leader* article about Fassett.

246. *Cleveland Leader*, March 5, 1874, 8, https://www.genealogybank.com/newspapers/sourcelist.

247. *Mahoning Valley Vindicator*, September 24, 1875, 5, https://news.google.com/newspapers?nid=sxPTjD2EoucC&dat=18750917.

248. "The Miners' National Convention," *Mahoning Vindicator*, October 24, 1873, 5, https://news.google.com/newspapers?nid=ib87rSy7x5MC&dat=18731024.

249. Frank Julian Warne, "The Union Movement among Coal Mine Workers," *Bulletin of the Bureau of Labor, Department of Commerce and Labor* (Washington, D.C.: Government Printing Office, March 1904), 382.

250. John S. Hittell, *The Commerce and Industries of the Pacific Coast of North America* (San Francisco: A.L. Bancroft and Company Publishers, 1882), 255, https://books.google.com/books?id=KH8rAQAAMAAJ.

251. "Laborers' Strike," *San Francisco Chronicle*, May 17, 1872, 3, https://www.genealogybank.com/newspapers/sourcelist.

252. "A Labor Strike—Violence Threatened," *San Francisco Evening Bulletin*, May 16, 1872, 3, https://www.genealogybank.com/newspapers/sourcelist.

253. "Long Island," *New York Tribune*, July 23, 1872, 8, https://www.genealogybank.com/newspapers/sourcelist.

254. "Trouble between the Irish and Italian Laborers in New York," *San Francisco Chronicle*, March 19, 1873, 2, https://www.genealogybank.com/newspapers/sourcelist.

255. "Will the Gas Men Strike?" *New York Herald*, March 25, 1873, 7, https://chroniclingamerica.loc.gov/lccn/sn83030313/1873-03-25/ed-1/seq-7/.

256. " 'Out' at Last: Strike of the Gasmen Begun in the Works of the New York Company," *New York Herald*, April 6, 1873, 14, https://chroniclingamerica.loc.gov/lccn/sn83030313/1873-04-06/ed-1/seq-14/.

257. Ibid.

258. Ibid.

259. Ibid.

260. "Dowsed Glims," *New York Herald*, April 8, 1873, 11, https://chroniclingamerica.loc.gov/lccn/sn83030313/1873-04-08/ed-1/seq-11/.

261. "Is This All Gas?" *New York Herald*, April 9, 1873, 7, https://chroniclingamerica.loc.gov/lccn/sn83030313/1873-04-09/ed-1/seq-7/.

262. Ibid.

263. "The Gas Famine Ended," *New York Herald*, April 12, 1873, 8, https://chroniclingamerica.loc.gov/lccn/sn83030313/1873-04-12/ed-1/seq-8/.

264. "The Moral of the Gas Strike," *New York Herald*, April 8, 1873, 11, https://chroniclingamerica.loc.gov/lccn/sn83030313/1873-04-08/ed-1/seq-11/.

265. "Italian Laborers," *Cincinnati Gazette,* June 25, 1874, 1, https://www.genealogybank.com/newspapers/sourcelist.

266. "War in the Pennsylvania Mines," *Richmond Daily Dispatch*, December 2, 1874, 2, https://chroniclingamerica.loc.gov/lccn/sn84024738/1874-12-02/ed-1/seq-2/.

267. Frank Cowan, "The Italians as Coal Miners," *Washington Reporter*, September 23, 1874, 3, https://www.genealogybank.com/newspapers/sourcelist.

268. "Dill as a Reformer: What a Workingman's Organ Thinks of Him," *Juanita (PA) Sentinel & Republican*, October 2, 1878, 8, https://chroniclingamerica.loc.gov/lccn/sn86053634/1878-10-02/ed-1/seq-8/.

269. *Cincinnati Daily Gazette*, September 30, 1874, 4, https://www.genealogybank.com/newspapers/sourcelist.

270. "War in the Pennsylvania Mines," *Richmond Daily Dispatch*.

271. "Tuscarawas Valley Coal Mining Troubles," *Cleveland Plain Dealer*, March 22, 1875, 4, https://www.genealogybank.com/newspapers/sourcelist.

272. "Meeting of Miners," *Cleveland Leader*, April 5, 1875, 6, https://www.genealogybank.com/newspapers/sourcelist.

273. "The Coal Strike," *Philadelphia Inquirer*, May 18, 1875, 1, https://www.genealogybank.com/newspapers/sourcelist.

274. *Wheeling (WV) Daily Intelligencer*, May 15, 1875, 2, https://chroniclingamerica.loc.gov/lccn/sn84026844/1875-05-15/ed-1/seq-2/.

275. "The Coal Strike," *Philadelphia Inquirer*.

276. "The Mining Troubles," *Alexandria Gazette*, May 18, 1875, 4, https://www.genealogybank.com/newspapers/sourcelist.

277. "Siney and Parks: The Verdict of the Jury!" *National Labor Tribune*, October 9, 1875, 1, https://www.genealogybank.com/newspapers/sourcelist.

278. Silvano Santini, *Una sintesi storica dell'industria mineraria in Italia* (Rome: self-published, 1996), 32, http://www.pionierieni.it/wp/wp-content/uploads/SNR-160-Storia-industria-mineraria-italiana-parte-prima.-S.-Santini-1996.pdf.

279. "The Miners' Conspiracy Trial," *New York Herald* (see n. 231).

280. *Labor Tribune*, quoted in "The Italian Miners," *Indianapolis Sentinel*, October 1, 1874, 7, https://www.genealogybank.com/newspapers/sourcelist.

281. "End of the Long Strike," *Indianapolis Sentinel,* June 16, 1875, 1, https://www.genealogybank.com/newspapers/sourcelist.

282. "The Lock-Out," *New York Herald*, November 17, 1874, 3, https://chroniclingamerica.loc.gov/lccn/sn83030313/1874-11-17/ed-1/seq-3/.

283. "Great Hocking Valley Coal Strike of 1884–1885," accessed May 9, 2019, http://www.ohiohistorycentral.org/w/Great_Hocking_Valley_Coal_Strike_of_1884-1885.

284. "Armed Invasion: A Body of Italians, under the Escort of an Armed Guard," *Cleveland Leader*, July 15, 1884, 1, https://www.genealogybank.com/newspapers/sourcelist.

285. "The War for Wages: Hocking Valley Hoodlums at Bay for a Time," *Philadelphia Inquirer*, September 2, 1884, 1, https://www.genealogybank.com/newspapers/sourcelist.

286. "Great Hocking Valley Coal Strike of 1884–1885," Topic Guide for Chronicling America, Ohio History Connection.

287. "Striking Quarrymen," *Saginaw Evening News*, April 2, 1886, 3, https://www.genealogybank.com/newspapers/sourcelist.

288. Between January and June 1873, over one hundred press reports appeared on the strike. Local newspapers, especially the *Mahoning Vindicator* and the *Western Reserve Chronicle*, covered the strike extensively. In addition, out-of-state dailies from San Francisco to Washington, D.C., followed the walkout.

289. "A Pittsburgher's Opinion of the Strike," *Canton Repository and Republican* (see n. 195).

290. "In the Mines," *Irish World and American Liberator*, January 30, 1892, 3, https://www.genealogybank.com/newspapers/sourcelist.

291. "An Evil Hard to Kill: The Padrone System Flourishing in the Coal Regions," *New Haven Register*, February 2, 1892, 1, https://www.genealogybank.com/newspapers/sourcelist.

292. "From Youngstown," *National Labor Tribune*, May 29, 1875, 2, https://www.genealogybank.com/newspapers/sourcelist.

293. Dr. Henry Louis Gates, message to authors, September 12, 2018.

294. Long, *Where the Sun Never Shines*, 202 (see n. 4).

295. Lewis, *Black Coal Miners in America*, 44 (see n. 160).

296. George R. Reiss, "Mill Operations Will Increase," *Youngstown Vindicator*, February 20, 1942, 25, https://news.google.com/newspapers?id=KeheAAAAIBAJ&sjid=5lMNAAAAIBAJ&pg=5203%2C6036896.

297. "Youngstown Paragraphs," *Mahoning Dispatch*, October 11, 1912, 1, https://chroniclingamerica.loc.gov/lccn/sn84028473/1912-10-11/ed-1/seq-1/.

298. U.S. Bureau of the Census, "Migration," 56–57 (see n. 71).

Chapter 9

299. J.R.A., "State Correspondence: Hubbard," *Cleveland Leader*, September 9, 1874, 7, https://www.genealogybank.com/newspapers/sourcelist.

300. Butler, *History of Youngstown*, 1:769–71 (see n. 42).

301. "The Mining Industry—Down in a Coal Mine," *Cleveland Leader*, July 7, 1879, 5, https://www.genealogybank.com/newspapers/sourcelist.

302. *History of Trumbull and Mahoning Counties* (Cleveland: H.Z. Williams & Bro., 1882), 2:365, https://books.google.com/books?id=SxoVAAAAYAAJ.

303. "The Mining Industry—Down in a Coal Mine," *Cleveland Leader*.

304 Butler, *History of Youngstown*, 2:81 (see n. 42).

305 Ibid.

306. "A Miners' Strike Threatened in the Mahoning Valley," *Stark County (OH) Democrat*, October 13, 1881, 1, https://chroniclingamerica.loc.gov/lccn/sn84028490/1881-10-13/ed-1/seq-1/.

307. Andrew Roy, "Strikes Reported by Coal Mines Employees that Occurred Since January 1, 1882," *Executive Documents: Annual Reports for 1882 made to the Governor, and Transmitted to the Sixty-Fifth General Assembly of the State of Ohio, at the Adjourned Session, Commencing January 2, 1883* (Columbus, OH: G.J. Brand & Co., 1883), 1407.

308. Family Search, "New York Passenger Lists, 1820–1891," accessed October 5, 2018, https://www.familysearch.org/ark:/61903/3:1:939V-RMKX-7?i=820&wc=MX6L-P38%3A165875901&cc=1849782.

309. Butler, *History of Youngstown*, 2:81 (see n. 42).

310. Ann N. Przelomski, "Sons of Sunny Italy Largest Unit Here," *Youngstown Vindicator*, April 29, 1951, A-22, https://news.google.com/newspapers?id=gt9RAAAAIBAJ&sjid=UoQMAAAAIBAJ&pg=1025%2C8686387.

311. Charles F. Carr, "Knowing Youngstown: Articles about Our City, Edited by the Public Library, No. 82: More about Youngstown's Italians," *Youngstown Daily Vindicator*, January 5, 1925, 11, https://news.google.com/newspapers?id=Tp5cAAAAIBAJ&sjid=EFgNAAAAIBAJ&pg=1104%2C1145874.

312. "Societa Fraterna Italiana," *Youngstown Evening Vindicator*, October 12, 1891, 1, https://news.google.com/newspapers?nid=MdMr--dQ_pMC&dat=18911012.

313. "Will Act as Interpreter," *Youngstown Evening Vindicator*, March 10, 1893, 2, https://news.google.com/newspapers?nid=MdMr--dQ_pMC&dat=18930310.

314. "An Opening," *Youngstown Daily Vindicator*, April 10, 1897, 3, https://news.google.com/newspapers?id=Sg9gAAAAIBAJ&sjid=NIEMAAAAIBAJ&pg=4073%2C7417824.

315. Butler, *History of Youngstown*, 2:151 (see n. 42).

316. Carr, "Knowing Youngstown."

317. "Big Offer," *Youngstown Daily Vindicator*, December 13, 1905, 4, https://news.google.com/newspapers?nid=pqgf-8x9CmQC&dat=19051213&printsec=frontpage&hl=en.

Chapter 10

318. Although it was a nickname, "Little Italy" appeared on the 1920 Hubbard census. The eastern boundary of the Italian neighborhood was marked by Greene Street. Glenn W. Lett, a Coalburg resident and the enumerator of the 1920 census, chose to denote the street as "Little Italy."

319. The Italian settlement included most of the Mahoning Coal Company's Addition to Coalburg, a twenty-two-acre tract of land on the eastern edge of Great Lot 22 in Hubbard Township. It was bounded on the east by Greene Street (later known as Bell Wick Road), on the south by Mount Everett Road, on the west by the Old Coal Road, and on the north by the northern boundary of Great Lot 22.

320. Appendix 10 identifies four of the 1880 Coalburg residents with four of the 1872 passengers on the SS *Erin*.

321. Carr, "Knowing Youngstown."

322. *Carovillesi* refers to residents of Carovilli.

323. Carr, "Knowing Youngstown."

324. Appendix 7 lists the Italians who arrived in Coalburg in March 1873.

325. Andrew Roy, *Fourth Annual Report of the State Mine Inspector to the Governor of the State of Ohio, for the Year 1877* (Columbus, OH: Nevins & Myers, State Printers, 1877), 70.

326. Family Search, "Ohio, County Births, 1841–2003," accessed October 5, 2018, https://www.familysearch.org/ark:/61903/3:1:33S7-9RK6-9NGW?i=57&wc=Q6QM-92N%3A227695801%2C227741801&cc=1932106.

327. Joseph Louis Sacchini, *The Italians of Youngstown and the Mahoning Valley, Ohio* (Baltimore: Gateway Press Inc., 1997), 185.

328. Donald B. Stough and John H. Curry, *Pioneer Days in Hubbard* (Hubbard, OH: self-published, 1940), 1.

329. Family Search, "Ohio, Trumbull County Records, 1795–2010."

330. Ibid.

331. "Landed in Jail: Report that Officers Arrest Angelo Will at Meadville," *Youngstown Vindicator*, February 26, 1898, 2, https://news.google.com/newspapers?id=nFZKAAAAIBAJ&sjid=D4YMAAAAIBAJ&pg=1577%2C3865488.

332. Butler, *History of Youngstown*, 2:372 (see n. 42).

333. "This Man's Name Is Angelo Parrella," interview with Andy Serafino, "Where Is He: The Italian Villain, Angelo Will, Not Yet Captured by Police," *Sunday Vindicator*, February 27, 1898, 3, https://news.google.com/newspapers?id=eQ1IAAAAIBAJ&sjid=34AMAAAAIBAJ&pg=4772%2C6097884.

334. "New Men Broke In," *Youngstown Vindicator*, April 11, 1907, 2, https://news.google.com/newspapers?id=wLJIAAAAIBAJ&sjid=foEMAAAAIBAJ&pg=5340%2C5996695.

335. "Ferrando Is Called Away," *Youngstown Vindicator*, March 27, 1919, 2.

336. Butler, *History of Youngstown*, 3:677–678 (see n. 42), https://hdl.handle.net/2027/nyp.33433081822706.

337. "News Section: Columbus," *Coal Trade Journal* 52, no. 41 (October 12, 1921), 1111, https://books.google.com/books?id=AkeOAytVZ9YC.

338. Family Search, "Ohio, Trumbull County Records, 1795–2010."

339. Family Search, "Ohio, County Births, 1841–2003."

340. From the civil records of Carovilli.

341. Ibid.

342. Family Search, "Ohio, County Marriages, 1789–2013," accessed October 5, 2018, https://www.familysearch.org/ark:/61903/3:1:9392-S53K-ZK?i=188&wc=Q6SP-FTP%3A122255401%2C122948501&cc=1614804.

343. Luke W. Bryan, "Annual Report of the Mine Inspector for the Indian Territory," in *Annual Reports of the Department of the Interior for the Fiscal Year ended June 30, 1899, vol. 2: Miscellaneous Reports* (Washington, D.C.: Government Printing Office, 1899), 764.

344. Kris Boyne, message to authors, January 25, 2018.

345. "Hubbard Pioneer Taken by Death," *Youngstown Vindicator*, August 20, 1921, 3, https://news.google.com/newspapers?id=E2ZKAAAAIBAJ&sjid=fYYMAAAAIBAJ&pg=4614%2C3981018.

346. N.J. Drohan, *History of Hubbard, Ohio Compiled by Rev. N.J. Drohan, Pastor St. Patrick's Church Hubbard, Ohio From Early Settlement in 1798 to 1907* (Hubbard, OH: self-published, 1907), 31.

347. Carr, "Knowing Youngstown" (see n. 311).

348. Jamie Metrailer, "Subiaco Abbey and Academy," Encyclopedia of Arkansas History and Culture, Butler Center for Arkansas Studies at the Central Arkansas Library System, http://www.encyclopediaofarkansas. net/encyclopedia/entry-detail.aspx?search=1&entryID=2523.

349. Family Search, "Arkansas Marriages, 1837–1944," accessed February 10, 2018, https://familysearch.org/ark:/61903/1:1:F73S-KW5.

350. U.S. Department of the Interior, Bureau of Land Management, General Land Office Records, Homestead Certificate 376, https:// glorecords.blm.gov/details/patent/default.aspx?accession=AR2040__.3 76&docClass=STA&sid=wmlqqcof.qu4#patentDetailsTabIndex=1.

351. "Coal Optimists Prepare for Winter," *Arkansas Gazette*, August 24, 1930, 33, https://www.genealogybank.com/newspapers/sourcelist.

352. Bill Izard, "A Southern Paris: Paris, Arkansas," PorterBriggs.com: The Voice of the South, 2015, http://porterbriggs.com/a-southern-paris-paris-arkansas/.

353. Arkansas Historic Preservation Program, National Register of Historic Places Registration Form, section 8, 7–8, October 1990, http://www. arkansaspreservation.com/National-Register-Listings/PDF/LO0270. nr.pdf.

354. Carr, "Knowing Youngstown" (see n. 311).

355. In Italy, the surname is spelled *Zarlenga* and *Zarlengo*. In the United States, versions of the name also include *Zarlinga* and even *Darling*!

356. William Ritezel, *Warren Western Reserve Chronicle*, May 21, 1873 (see n. 208).

357. *Cleveland Daily Plain Dealer*, May 21, 1873, 2, https://www.genealogybank. com/newspapers/sourcelist.

358. Family Search, "Ohio, County Marriages, 1789–2013" (see n. 342).

359. Ibid.

360. *Ohio Patriot*, May 23, 1873, 3, http://lepper.advantage-preservation. com/Viewer/?k=dangelo&i=f&by=1873&bdd=1870&d=01011873-12311873&m=between&fn=ohio_patriot_usa_ohio_new_lisbon_18730523_english_3&df=1&dt=1.

361. Roy, *Fourth Annual Report*, 170 (see n. 325).

362. Ibid., 171.

363. A map of Mahoning Mine Number 3, showing its intricate system of underground passages, can be seen in Appendix 11.

364. Carr, "Knowing Youngstown" (see n. 311).

365. Family Search, "Ohio, County Marriages, 1789–2013" (see n. 342).

366. "Some Eating," *Mahoning Vindicator*, May 23, 1873, 5, https://news.google.com/newspapers?nid=ib87rSy7x5MC&dat=18730523.

367. U.S. Bureau of the Census, "Migration," 57 (see n. 71).

368. Cowan, "The Italians as Coal Miners," *Washington Reporter* (see n. 267).

Appendix 1

369. "The Coal Miners Strike," *Cleveland Daily Leader*, January 30, 1873, 4, https://www.genealogybank.com/newspapers/sourcelist.

370. Przelomski, "Sons of Sunny Italy Largest Unit Here," *Youngstown Vindicator* (see n. 310).

371. Butler, *History of Youngstown*, 2:151 (see n. 42).

372. Howard C. Aley, *A Heritage to Share: The Bicentennial History of Youngstown and Mahoning County, Ohio, From Prehistoric Times to the National Bicentennial Year* (Youngstown, OH: Youngstown Lithographing Company, 1975), 50.

Appendix 2

373. *Post Office Directory: List of Post Offices in the United States: Revised and Corrected to the Post Office Department, to Sept. 1, 1870* (Washington, D.C.: Government Printing Office, September 1, 1870), 44, https://hdl.handle.net/2027/hvd.32044036304590.

374. John S. Gallagher and Alan H. Patera, *The Post Offices of Ohio* (Burtonsville, MD: The Depot, 1979).

375. Family Search, "United States Census, 1940," accessed October 5, 2018, https://www.familysearch.org/ark:/61903/3:1:3QSQ-G9M1-7HFN?i=10&cc=2000219.

Appendix 3

376. "Effect of Discovery of Coal Was Influential," *Hubbard News*, September 13, 1934, 15.

Appendix 4

377. "Increase of Italian Emigration to the United States," *New York Herald*, September 3, 1872, 6, https://chroniclingamerica.loc.gov/lccn/sn83030313/1872-09-03/ed-1/seq-6/.

378. "A Remarkable Swindle," *New York Tribune*, November 23, 1872, 1, https://chroniclingamerica.loc.gov/lccn/sn83030214/1872-11-23/ed-1/seq-1/.

379. "The Pauper Italians," *New York Herald* (see n. 81).

380. "Emigrants' Wrongs," *New York Tribune* (see n. 86).

381. Ibid.

382. *Boston Daily Advertiser*, November 25, 1872, 2, https://www.genealogybank.com/newspapers/sourcelist.

383. "A Remarkable Swindle," *New York Tribune*.

384. "The Pauper Italians," *New York Herald* (see n. 81).

385. "The Italian Emigrants," *New York Herald* (see n. 72).

386. "Italian Immigrants," *New York Herald*, December 16, 1872, 10, https://chroniclingamerica.loc.gov/lccn/sn83030313/1872-12-16/ed-1/seq-10/.

387. "Arrivals," *New York Herald*, November 8, 1872, 10, https://chroniclingamerica.loc.gov/lccn/sn83030313/1872-11-08/ed-1/seq-10/.

388. "Arrivals," *New York Herald*, December 12, 1872, 10, https://chroniclingamerica.loc.gov/lccn/sn83030313/1872-12-12/ed-1/seq-10/.

389. "More Italians," *New York Herald*, January 5, 1873, 4, https://chroniclingamerica.loc.gov/lccn/sn83030313/1873-01-05/ed-1/seq-4/.

390. *New York Herald*, January 5, 1873, 10, https://chroniclingamerica.loc.gov/lccn/sn83030313/1873-01-05/ed-1/seq-10/.

391. "Pauper Immigration," *Emporia (KS) News*, December 27, 1872, 2, https://chroniclingamerica.loc.gov/lccn/sn82016419/1872-12-27/ed-1/seq-2/.

392. "The Immigrant Italians: What Caused Them to Leave Sunny Italy for America," *New York Herald*, January 3, 1873, 10, https://chroniclingamerica.loc.gov/lccn/sn83030313/1873-01-03/ed-1/seq-10/.

393. "Gentlemen of Genoa," *New York Herald*, January 2, 1873, 7, https://chroniclingamerica.loc.gov/lccn/sn83030313/1873-01-02/ed-1/seq-7/.

394. "Starvation at Sea," *New York Sun*, January 2, 1873, 2, https://chroniclingamerica.loc.gov/lccn/sn83030272/1873-01-02/ed-1/seq-2/.

395. "A Remarkable Swindle," *New York Tribune*.

396. "The Italians: More of the Emigrant Machinery—Work Wanted for Willing Men," *New York Herald*, January 4, 1873, 8, https://chroniclingamerica.loc.gov/lccn/sn83030313/1873-01-04/ed-1/seq-8/.

Appendix 10

397. "Funerals," *Youngstown Vindicator*, January 7, 1929, 19.

398. "A Murder Trial: On This Week—An Italian Who Sought to Wipe Out a Family," *Warren Western Reserve Chronicle*, May 17, 1898, 8.

INDEX

ABOUT THE AUTHORS

Ben Lariccia, a native of Youngstown, is a public historian and writer in the area of Italian American history. He has a bachelor's degree from the University of Dayton and a master's degree in bilingual/bicultural education from La Salle University. For thirty years, he taught in the School District of Philadelphia. Ben is a contributing writer at *La Gazzetta Italiana* newspaper. His work is also published in print and online by the Italian group Amici di Capracotta. He is a member of the America-Italy Society of Philadelphia and the Italian American Studies Association.

Joe Tucciarone was born in Youngstown and raised in nearby Hubbard. He earned a bachelor of science degree from Youngstown State University and a master's degree from the University of Toledo. In 2000, he was awarded an honorary doctorate of science from Youngstown State University. His astronomical animations have appeared in dozens of Discovery and National Geographic Channel documentaries, and his illustrations enhance the covers of several books, including *When the Sun Dies* and *Night Comes to the Cretaceous*. *La Gazzetta Italiana* recently published Joe's article "The First Italians in Trumbull County, Ohio."